Legacy by Design

Succession Planning for Agribusiness Owners

Legacy by Design

Succession Planning for Agribusiness Owners

Kevin Spafford

Marketplace Books
Columbia Maryland

This publication is designed to provide accurate and authoritative information in regard to the subject matter covered. It is sold with the understanding that neither the author nor the publisher is engaged in rendering legal, accounting, or other professional service. If legal advice or other expert assistance is required, the services of a competent professional person should be sought.

From a Declaration of Principles jointly adopted by a Committee of the American Bar Association and a Committee of Publishers.

This book, along with other books, is available at discounts that make it realistic to provide them as gifts to your customers, clients, and staff. For more information on these long lasting, cost effective premiums, please call us at 800-272-2855 or e-mail us at sales@fpbooks.com.

ISBN 1-59280-214-1

Printed in the United States of America.

1 2 3 4 5 6 7 8 9 0

TABLE OF CONTENTS

ACKNOWLEDGMENTS

Though we may pride ourselves on independence and self-reliance, we reach a stage in life when we realize that, if not for those who walk beside us, nothing great would ever be accomplished.

Because of the unbelievable demands of writing this book, and every other challenging endeavor through which I have put my family, I thank my wife Anne-Marie, my son Drew, and my daughter Sara, for their inspiration and unyielding support. They stood at the ready with kind words of encouragement, motivating challenges for results, and a warm home as a safe haven.

Nothing great is ever created solo. It takes a cast of characters, each playing a part to inspire and support big efforts. It is my pleasure to thank Mike McGarvey for his incredible art work, Nancy Acheson for her constant support, John D'Ewart for his legal oversight, Larry Chambers for being an excellent writing coach, and Karen Johnson and Mayo Morely for their editorial work.

It was an immense pleasure to interview so many fine and generous people. The time people gave and the personal stories they shared helped to inform and shape this book. Thanks to the farmers, agribusiness owners, and friends listed below who encouraged my search for the truth:

Glenn and Zetti Aldridge
Nick Bertagna
Eric Black
Bruce Book
Mike Bryant
Rodney Carter
Ira Compton
Bill Eiler
Bruce Fiock
Jim and Iola Gibson
George Gomes
Jim Granzella
Charlie Hawes
Bob Hennigan
Ben Hillebrecht
Tim and Reggie Hunzeker
John and Laura Kapusnik
Robert Kidd
Dax & Karen Kimmelshue

Mark Kimmelshue
Leo and Linda Langerwerf
Roger Loftus
David Lohse
John Lohse
Tom Martin
Tony Martinez
Ed McLaughlin
Jim Mead
Mark Montgomery
Sara Mora
Myron Openshaw
Martin and Sally Pozzi
Steve Prentice
Dave and Jane Roberti
Roger Sohnrey
Jim Williams
Dan Woolery

DEDICATION

Dedicated to our most valuable citizens: "Cultivators of the earth are the most valuable citizens. They are the most vigorous, the most independent, the most virtuous. And they are tied to their country, and wedded to its liberty and interests, by the most lasting bonds."

Thomas Jefferson

The letter is from The Life and Selected Writings of Thomas Jefferson. Edited by Adrienne Koch and William Peden. New York: Random House, 1972, p 377.

INTRODUCTION

Is the Family Farm Doomed to Extinction?

Of the 2.13 million farms in the United States, 99% are owned by individuals, family partnerships, or family corporations. Of these, 30% may pass to a second gen-eration, but less than 10% will pass to a third. The three leading causes of failure to pass the family farm to the next generation include:

- Inadequate estate planning,
- Insufficient capitalization, and
- Failure to prepare the next generation properly.

A family business, be it a farm, an agribusiness, or a factory, is like the proverbial "elephant in the living room." We all see it, and know it is going to make a big mess, but no one mentions it. In the scores of personal surveys with farmers and agribusiness owners over the years, I found the following:

- Only 36% of the farmers and agribusiness owners had some form of estate plan.
- A total of 82% of farmers did not have an exit plan, nor did they know how to create one.
- Only 12% had a retirement plan in place, while 88% planned on the generosity of the government or the grace of God.

In 47.7% of failure scenarios, the collapse of the family business occurred after the founder's death (according to Family Firm Institute 2002), usually due to insufficient capital.

These are dismal statistics, yet I truly believe they can improve. A lack of communication is a direct factor in the failure to pass business interests to the next generation. In fact, a failure to communicate affects much, much, more. One former agribusiness owner assured me that "communication is the heartbeat of a family business." Without constructive, consistent communication there is no way to grow a business. Communication among the generations regarding the tough issues involved in succession planning is often ignored or brushed over as something that can wait. The refrain I most often associate with this attitude is, "It's important, but we have work to do..."

Case Study

His situation seemed simple enough. Wendell Satterly, a widower with two sons and a daughter, owned a large timber ranch in Northern California. When the time came for Wendell to retire, he hired multiple advisors and spent a considerable amount of time and money crafting a succession plan. He said it included an ownership succession plan and an estate plan; however, his retirement plan never did materialize and no one discussed the business itself.

After finishing small talk, Wendell slid a file across the table. It contained the action agreements, organ-ized into brightly-colored folders. I flipped open the folder labeled "succession" and began to question Wendell about the plans. He looked perplexed as he explained that this part of the plan did not turn out as he had hoped. I asked how his children responded during the initial family consultation. "Family consultation?" Wendell replied in puzzled tones.

It seems that Wendell made the common mistake of assuming that his eldest son would naturally want to take over the business. "How could he not?", Wendell asked, with the puzzlement of a person who has been living out his dream.

I learned that neither son shared Wendell's dream. The oldest son had no interest in timber man-agement and, instead, wanted to become a doctor. The younger son hoped to move away from the isolation of the ranch and was more interested in living in a large city and becoming an actor.

As it turned out, no one had communicated with the children until after the plans were written. The family was not consulted at all during the planning phase of the plan. Everyone rushed head-long into design and technique, and no one bothered to ask if this is what was best for the family. As is often the case, it was much easier, but completely ineffective, to assume rather than to communicate.

Wendell's daughter had married, and although her husband Ray was a hardworking guy in his late twenties, Wendell had never even considered them as viable succession candidates to run the farm. Patty loved the farm and wanted nothing more than to stay there and help it prosper.

We explored the opportunity of designing a real plan to pass the ownership to Patty and Ray. We involved the entire family, and integrated the estate plan and

> a retirement plan. The plans provided financial security for Wendell, yet left plenty of capital to support the business operation. Both sons were included in the plan as primary beneficiaries on life insurance policies designed to provide equitable benefits.
>
> We worked out a true comprehensive succession solution — a solution measured against what is best for the family, the business, and Wendell — a solution we established through open communication.

Farming is the quintessential family business. No other business endeavor is as emotionally charged as the family farm. Improving the communication necessary for comprehensive succession planning for America's agricultural industry can potentially affect every family-owned farm or agribusiness in America.

Many of the business people I met completed some pieces of a succession plan, usually in the form of estate planning. Yet, they often hesitated to share the information with all family members and rarely was this information up-to-date. Many of those individuals who had completed some estate planning felt reasonably comfortable until I started asking questions.

My mission is to make a difference and to improve the dismal statistical dead-end awaiting most family-owned businesses. If I can help just one family keep the farm—a farm that may otherwise be lost due to a lack of preparation, insufficient capital, or a hesitancy to communicate—I will fulfill the objective of this book. If I can help families to open discussions regarding succession planning, I will have accomplished my mission.

PILLARS THAT SUPPORT A COMPREHENSIVE SUCCESSION PLAN

Comprehensive succession planning is the foundation upon which a successful multigenerational family-owned business is built. There are four distinct pillars that support a comprehensive succession plan: business planning, ownership succession, estate planning, and retirement planning. Each phase of the plan is measured by what is best for you, your family, and your business. Decisions can be made very easily when only judged by one or two factors, but comprehensive succession planning must consider all four as equally important. The decisions made by the partners in a family-owned business affect many people. Actions made wisely today can benefit several generations in the future.

Business Planning

A well-written business plan begins with a vision of how the business should look, act, and feel and is designed to bring this vision to fruition. A complete plan includes a detailed exploration of opportunities for development. Each goal or objective is supported by specific action steps. A budget not only shows a bottom line but also acts as a measuring stick for progress.

Ownership Succession

A written commitment ideally details who, when, and under what conditions management and ownership responsibilities are left to succeeding generations. A complete plan enhances business stability, promotes growth opportunities, communicates confidence to third parties, and develops leadership for the next generation.

Estate Planning

A written plan, supported by legal and accounting issues, to transfer assets and property to the next generation is the most efficient and cost-effective method. Estate planning ensures that the farm passes to heirs unencumbered by debt that may threaten the viability of the farm business.

Retirement and Financial Independence Planning

Many farmers are woefully unprepared for life's prolonged second half. The average length of retirement is 20 years and quickly approaching 30. Can you afford financial independence for 20 to 30 years? This expanded life expectancy gives people time to chart a new course. Financial planning acts as the cornerstone, giving strength to your succession foundation.

WHY SUCCESSION PLANNING?

Comprehensive succession planning is about what is best for the family-owned business. What is best for the business may seem easy at first glance, but each business is a unique blend of people, history, experiences, and expectations. The number of lives touched through a family business may be significantly greater than anyone cares to admit.

Case Study

Grandpa bought a 500-acre farm containing the best bottom land in the valley for $200 an acre in 1911. When dad acquired the farm a few decades later, it had a value of $500 per acre. Through the power of a will and the meager estate planning grandpa did, dad owned the farm out-right. His two sisters were left with some other less important assets, and dad supported his mother with the farm income. Though this situation may have been acceptable in the 1930s, today that same farm is quite possibly worth several million dollars, depending on the county and state in which it is located. There are more people involved and a plethora of self interests. Farms are no longer just passed from dad to the eldest son. Though the simplicity of that era is enviable, no one today would consider such a solution.

Fast-forward to today. Dad dies, and his son assumes the management role on the farm. The second son practices law in the city, and a sister is raising a family and supporting her family's business in another state. The farm is now divided three ways: the son who works the farm (active participant) is responsible for his mother and the entire farming operation. He must maintain, if not grow, the farm business, manage the farm assets, look after his mother, and consult his siblings (inactive partners). His job, his career choice, and everything for which he has worked has just become more complicated. Decisions that used to be made by him and dad, two committed active participants, are now made through long-distance consultations with inactive partners. It is likely that both active and inactive partners have opposing objectives for the farm, especially in relation to the income. Active partners want to grow the farm business. They want to see money reinvested into production and capital expenditures, which enhance the long-term business profit. Inactive partners often want to realize net income. They want to see a return on their investment, an investment that appears significant in the net worth column on their balance sheet but which has virtually no value on the open market unless the farm is sold. An attitude of animosity can prevail between active and inactive partners.

What is Comprehensive Succession Planning?

Comprehensive succession planning strategically prepares the farm business for the inevitable transfer of ownership. A comprehensive succession plan may require a multi-disciplinary team of professionals, including a financial planner, an attorney, an accountant, and possibly a banker among others. It involves planning and advice for multiple generations of the family. It includes financial, estate, retirement, and business planning.

The entire process is predicated on goals; these goals shape your succession plan. It may involve an extensive discovery process, soul searching, and commitment. Some common goals may include:

- Financial security in retirement
- Providing for dependents
- Ensuring that the farm remains in the family
- Treating the children equitably and fairly (there is a difference).

How to Use This Book

I recommend that you grab a pen and a highlighter. As you read each section, highlight areas of interest to you. Use the pen to note questions and concerns in the margins. This book is designed as a working guide, so put it to good use. This book is not a course designed to make a short trip out of what can otherwise be an endless journey. It is designed as a wake-up call, a gentle encouragement for you to take action and to stop putting off that conversation with a financial planner, an attorney, or an accountant.

part 1
VISION TO REALITY
business planning

In this section, the focus is on creating a vision and designing a plan to bring this vision to reality. Some questions to ask yourself follow:

- What will your legacy be?
- Will it be a stewardship of the family land?
- Will it be the wealth you have accumulated?
- Or will it entail future opportunities for earning that the farm represents?
- Perhaps it is the values you cherish such as hard work, honesty, and independence—the values represented by the development of your farm, which you hope to leave to your children.

The answers to these issues form the foundation of your vision—that is, knowing whether or not you are effectively leaving the things you value most to subsequent generations.

This section also focuses on the first element of creating a comprehensive succession plan—that is, a well-written business plan. A business plan is nothing more than written instructions for bringing your vision to reality. To record your vision, you must have one. You need a sense of the future. A complete business plan includes a thorough analysis of your current situation, as well as a detailed exploration of future opportunities for development. The business plan also details the actions necessary to realize your objectives. It is a measuring stick for checking your progress.

In this book, a planning sequence - a Comprehensive Succession Solution - was designed specifically to help you accomplish your objectives.

As a farm/agribusiness owner, you may at times feel as though your farm is like another member of the family. It is rewarding in a challenging yet satisfying way. The attachment that you feel for the farm is at times very motivating. It is like a child, you want to see it do well. At other times it constricts your options, as you do not want to see it harmed. The emotions that support your conviction are a blessing and a curse.

Some of the most common goals of farm/agribusiness owners include:

1. Maintaining family ownership
2. Passing a viable business opportunity to the next generation
3. Developing a nest egg for retirement or for the next venture in one's vocational life
4. Leaving the family and dependents financially secure
5. Minimizing tax liabilities and transfer obligations
6. Most importantly, doing what is best for the family and the business

Addressing these, at times, conflicting goals may be among the biggest challenges you face.

Case Study

The owner of an agribusiness, already in its second generation, is concerned about the transfer to the next generation. He wants the business to be transferred to his son, but he does not want to exclude his other children from his estate. First he wrote a business plan to solidify the operation, and then he identified the skills and abilities needed to run the business. After measuring the management skills required against his son's current abilities, he was able to create a personal development plan for his son. A non-family mentor was appointed to help the son implement his plan. It was monitored on a quarterly basis. The assessment of the business helped to identify the need for an updated inventory system, among other things. After two years of implementing the succession plan, areas of responsibility gradually changed hands. When the owner dies, his son will be given the opportunity to inherit part of the agribusiness and purchase the remainder. The owner's goals and objectives were met. They were achieved by following a planning sequence designed to protect the family farm. The owner was able to avoid unnecessary transfer obligations, provide adequate capital, and prepare the next generation to assume a leadership role. Besides leaving the family farm, something else very important was achieved. The owner found a way to treat his children equitably and fairly (and there is a difference).

chapter 1
YOUR LEGACY

The legacy specifically addressed here is the desire to pass a viable business opportunity to the succeeding generation. Your agricultural business enterprise is your life's work, your estate, your retirement plan, and your legacy to succeeding generations. As your creation, it is a reflection of all that you hold dear. Since reality dictates that we are all stewards of our lifetime possessions, every business entity yields control of ownership to the next generation or dissolves. The objective throughout this book is to ensure that your legacy is your design.

Take the time to evaluate what you want to leave, how you want to leave it, and to whom. The beginning point of this decision is a vision, a clear picture of the future you want to create. To clarify and prioritize your personal goals, complete the following exercises.

VISION STATEMENT EXERCISE

Create Lists

Vision becomes reality through the judicious investment of time. In the book How to Get Control of Your Time and Your Life, Alan Lakein recommends a simple yet revealing exercise. He recommends writing a lifelong goal statement. Borrowing this concept, it is suggested that you use a similar exercise to create a vision statement. This important statement encompasses all of the goals and accomplishments you want to achieve in your lifetime. Take out a few sheets of paper, a pencil, and a watch. At the top of the first sheet of paper write the following:

What do I want to achieve during my lifetime?

Allow yourself to think about everything you have ever wanted to accomplish. Now take exactly two minutes to list every goal or objective that comes to mind. At this point you are not to second-guess yourself nor should you hesitate a moment to judge any of the entries.

This is an invitation to write just what you think you have always wanted. Through this exercise you will discover what is really important to you. You will uncover long-term aspirations, deeply buried dreams, and maybe some outlandish desires. Just write what comes to mind. From a long-term perspective, what do you want to accomplish during your lifetime?

Allow yourself another two minutes to review and edit the list. How important are your objectives? Which ones jump out as long-held and heartfelt beliefs? Which entries are superfluous, trivial, or inconsequential? The purpose at this point is to get a big-picture perspective of your most important lifetime goals.

On the next sheet of paper write the following:

What would I like to accomplish over the next three years?

Again, allow yourself two minutes to write your list and two minutes to review and edit it. Again, list everything that comes to mind, as quickly as possible. You may notice a pattern or similarities between the two lists. Depending on your age, the three-year time limit will make you factor in varying levels of urgency. As you age, you realize how fast three years can pass. Conversely, you realize that many important goals can be started or even accomplished during that period. Remember, this is not the time for judgment. Editing the list has one simple purpose, to delete any entry that does not fit.

The title of the third sheet of paper should read,

> *If I had only six months to live, what*
> *would I want to accomplish?*

Again, allow yourself two minutes to make a list and two minutes to review and edit it. In answering this question, do not focus on the details of funerals, wills, or estate settlements. Instead, think of what you want to accomplish in the short-term.

Now place the three lists in front of you. At first preview, you may be astounded at how accurately you captured some of the objectives that heretofore may not have been conscious thoughts. There will be deep-felt, or long sought after, goals listed on each page. Until you actually see these goals written down in your own handwriting, you may hesitate to admit how important certain accomplishments really are. It is amazing the distance some people go to avoid doing the activities they know will bring them closer to a lifetime goal. Most people are very cognizant of the extra effort necessary to fulfill a lifetime goal. My job as coach is to hold up a figurative mirror and allow you to see for yourself what you really want. I also want you to see the excuses you may use to avoid having to exert the concentrated effort to achieve your true desires.

Prioritize Your Goals

The next step in the vision statement process is to prioritize your goals. Prioritizing your goals after you make the initial list is critical. As you review each list ask yourself:

- What do I want?
- When do I want it?
- In what am I willing to invest?
- What sacrifices am I willing to make in order to get what I want?

Note the top three priorities from each of the three lists. At this point, you will begin to see a picture of the life you want to create. This picture serves as the basis of the vision you will create when you complete this exercise.

Your vision will become the foundation on which all future plans are built. As you progress through the factors included in a comprehensive succession plan, you will often refer to your vision. Vision gives direction. Vision insures alignment between objectives and action. Vision serves as the rudder that steers the ship.

Write A Vision Statement

Determine which goals or objectives are most important to you on a short- and a long-term basis. The list of goals—given six months to live   may deserve careful consideration. These goals may point to areas that are urgent. Take time now to write a vision statement. Write an essay predicting what the future promises based on what you want to accomplish. The essay that you write reflects your life in the future given the plans that you make based on the goals that you set. The essay is your own design for your reference. Feel relaxed about writing in your own style. Alternatively, you may simply list your goals and objectives as bullet points.

In order for a vision to come to fruition it must be shared. You must be willing to share your vision with those people who can help you in its achievement. Nothing is ever accomplished by a single individual. It takes teams of people to achieve the great accomplishments in life. Your business is no exception. In an interdependent society, multiple people, ideas, and resources may be required in order to accomplish a goal. The more clearly you write your vision, the easier it will be to share. When speaking of sharing your vision, you do not necessarily have to allow another person to read it. It may contain entries that are very personal. However, you must be able to articulate it. The process of writing your vision starts in your heart. It is pictured in your mind and then written. The process of writing forces you to clarify. In that clarification, you will begin to see where others will be instrumental in helping you.

This exercise, when completed sincerely, allows you to see clearly the direct connection between you and your work. If you are true to yourself, you cannot separate the at-work you from the at-home you. The values and principals that guide your life are not subject to working hours.

chapter 2
MAXIMIZE THE RETURN ON THE BUSINESS

From a succession planning standpoint, business valuation is a double-edged sword. On the one hand, you want to maximize your business value through sweat equity, capital investment, and market development. On the other hand, from an estate planning standpoint, you want to minimize the value as estate taxes and transfer obligations are all predicated on the value of the business in your gross estate.

Business valuation is about establishing a business value today, projecting a future value based on development potential and appreciation, then using a business plan to reach the potential value. Business valuation affects many of the decisions you make in your succession plan. The value of your farm establishes a purchase price for your buy/sell agreement. It helps you design a plan for lifetime gifts, private annuity sales, self-canceling installment notes (notes that cancel upon the death of the note holder), recapitalizations, and limited partnership interests. Accurate valuation helps to establish values for equitable distribution to your children. Thus, the value of your farm plays a big role in your estate planning strategies.

Valuation can mean many things to many people. Your efforts should be focused on ensuring that you maximize the appraised value of the business entity that you are developing. Maximizing the return on your investment should be an important focus of your business operation.

BUSINESS VALUATION

The Internal Revenue Code (rev. rule 59-60) uses the following definition of fair market value:

"...the net amount which a willing purchaser...would pay for the interest to a willing seller, neither being under any compulsion to buy or to sell and both having reasonable knowledge of the facts."

There is a significant difference between leaving a business and leaving the assets of a business to the next generation. A business by nature is an entity in and of itself with value—that is, an ongoing concern with real customers, employees, and products. The assets of a business may consist of land, buildings, lease holdings, equipment, and production inputs. An ongoing business carries significantly higher value than the parts and pieces of a former business.

The value of a farm or agribusiness then is based on what the business owns and what the business earns. A farm can be valued according to three definitions of business assets: as parts and pieces that can be sold separately, as an ongoing concern, and as a growth opportunity.

Parts And Pieces

Assets of a business—land, equipment, lease holdings, and production inputs—are usually sold piecemeal and at less than desired values, when the business has not been successful. This is often referred to as a liquidation, whereby assets are sold and operations generally cease. Monies earned from the sale often are needed to pay expenses and debt.

An Ongoing Concern

The second valuation of a farm or agribusiness is as an ongoing concern. The value of assets is based on the value of the agricultural output as well as certain intangibles such as training, experienced work force, systems/procedures, and current customers. Most family operations fit into this category. As long as the operation is consistently managed and diligently worked, business continues as usual. Growth can happen, but it is usually the result of acquiring an adjacent property or expanding into custom work.

Growth Opportunity

The third valuation alternative is a business with unique systems, specific procedures, and customer expectations. A business such as this most likely has a customer base, marketing systems, and a proprietary customer engagement model. It offers the owner an excellent business opportunity. The owner learns the existing business and then continues to develop and grow. The book value of such a business refers to assets of the business adjusted for depreciation, amortization, and unrealized losses.

MONETARY BENEFITS

A business with a clear and complete business plan is perceived as well managed. It increases in value because it has a consistent approach to marketing and operational issues. Income projections allow business management to make educated decisions about production inputs and alternative investments to grow the business and new systems to develop other products.

A business plan promotes analysis and an honest look at new opportunities. In addition, the process of writing a comprehensive business plan allows you to take a microscopic look at all aspects of your business.

- Are there areas for improvement?
- Should we replace equipment that currently takes two operators with a new one with an advanced design that only requires one operator?
- Do opportunities exist within the business climate to develop a new product?
- Are customers asking for a product they assume would be a complement to our current product line?
- Can you diversify your offering or integrate other markets?
- Are there better systems available, or can you streamline what is today an operational speed bump?
- Can you better focus employee action or should you improve employee skills and abilities?
- Are you exercising good expense management or can you improve your investment results?

Creating a business plan forces you to review closely your financial situation, resources, and commitments, and, in some cases, to ferret out unnecessary expenditures.

As a roadmap is used for a trip across the country, a business plan gives clear direction. A well-written business plan does not allow room for misinterpretation of the goals or intentions of the business owner. It is written so clearly that even a beginner in the business can follow the directions and succeed. A business plan allows you the opportunity to plan reviews and measure progress at any given in the production year.

NON-MONETARY BENEFITS

Anything that affects good business management affects the bottom-line. Good business communication involves clearly defined goals, shared values, and business principles. All of these lead to consistent business results. A well-written business plan reinforces the importance of an organized process for conducting business.

Communication is the heartbeat of any family business and is enhanced by a well-written business plan.

A business plan offers guidance to management. A blueprint is to contractors what a business plan is to your organizational team. When decisions need to be made, consulting a business plan helps to clarify and reinforce previously defined business objectives. Each business manager has a clear choice. He can operate by design or by default. If you know what you want to achieve and you have certain objectives, then decisions are easy. You either take the action necessary to fulfill your objectives or you do not.

A business with shared values is always more successful than a business without. A business plan offers the opportunity to think through the values that you as a proprietor want to see replicated. Once written, you have the opportunity to review exactly the values and attitudes you want represented by your business, your actions, and the actions of those associated with your business.

The act of sharing and reinforcing those written values on a regular basis with family and employees serves to perpetuate what is most important.

Every business plan contains objective measures of results. Goals are specifically enumerated to measure the level of success for a given period, usually a year. Clearly defined goals become the backbone of all business activity. Once a goal or objective is set, then all activity and all decisions are dedicated to its achievement. Your actions, investments, and methods are all designed to support the goals in your business plan.

SUMMARY

The way to affect the value of a business is to change what it owns and what it earns. Business owners can change these two factors through the decisions that you make. Through careful planning and consistent execution your agribusiness operation can grow to become whatever you want. If you can dream it, you can do it. The following factors are influenced through careful planning, consistent execution, and unwavering focus.

- The size of your business: Are you taking advantage of economies of scale?
- The growth/reduction trends: Is your business trending up or down?
- The products/services offered: Are you expanding your product line, specializing or developing a proprietary product?
- Diversity of operation: Are you vertically or horizontally integrating your market?
- Is the industry or commodity trending positive or negative?

Are you competitively positioned in this industry? Is there room for growth/development within the industry or commodity group?

- Is valuation based on current/projected earnings? (This is a very important factor since this is the business' raison d'etre.)
- What is the value of the business based on a moderate capitalization rate? Does the return warrant the investment?
- Is the goodwill/name/reputation of the business worth a premium over and above other similarly valued companies?
- Do you have an easily recognized brand, status, or prestige?

There are many factors that affect the value of a business. The important point is that you as the owner can change most of them. Business planning allows you to alter the value of your business operation.

chapter 3
BUSINESS GROWTH AND DEVELOPMENT

For the last century, the agricultural industry has been governed by commodity pricing. Agriculture is the pre-eminent commodity industry. Not only is the physical product a commodity, but the entire industry serves a commoditized business model. Commodity is the entire focus of the food market. Differentiation means a product would not sell or was unacceptable to wholesalers. Any recognizable difference in product, be it size, color or taste, would render that product unacceptable in a commodity market. As profits thin and costs of production rise, a farmer must find a better business model in order to survive.

Growth and Development through Vertical Integration

Vertical integration may present a viable solution for growing a business. Rather than fighting the market, farmers must create an integrated means to the market by controlling more of the steps from "farm gate to dinner plate." Farmers can develop a means of integration by, for example, purchasing a subsidiary, establishing a contractual relationship with an outsource company, or forming a strategic alliance. Combining resources with other farmers may offer an opportunity to modify your business model, impact the market, and tip the economies of scale in your favor.

On November 8, 2004, an article entitled "Moving On Up, Agricultural Firms Are Looking for a New Growth Model. They're Hoping it's Vertical Integration" appeared in the Wall Street Journal. This article stated that "no other American industry has to work so hard to find new ways to grow." Because of the many constraints, regulations, and uncertainties of agriculture, it is often difficult to see the opportunities. Increasing the breadth of your operation through vertical integration may provide the necessary economic opportunities.

> ### Case Study
> Kathy and Paul are excellent sheep ranchers; they care for their flock as if the sheep were part of the family. From sunrise to sunset everything they do is dedicated to the health, safety, and growth of the herd. Kathy spends all day in the fields moving stock from one field to the next to ensure the most nutritious feed. She watches the flock and protects the young lambs; she fixes fences and tends to sick animals. Paul is the consummate salesperson; he is either on the phone or knocking on doors of the best restaurants in San Francisco marketing their lamb.

If all farmers, and in fact all business owners, suffer from the same constraints, it is reasonable to suppose that those who rise to the challenge will be positioned to profit. Agriculture is going through some very significant upheavals. Farmers' earnings are squeezed today as never before. You are asked to do more with less. Input costs increase as commodity prices decline. Foreign competition exerts pricing pressures on all commodities. There seems to be a never-ending string of bureaucratic challenges each grower must navigate before applying many of the fertilizer or herbicide inputs that make agricultural practices so prolific. Automation which promotes efficiency in agricultural practices also increases capital expenditure.

A futurist might deduce that the next frontier for the agricultural enterprise is to focus on the soft qualities of business such as people, ideas, relationships, and flexibility. Most agricultural enterprises are built to satisfy the hard, impersonal, market-driven, commodity producing and stable environment of the past. Tom Peters, management consultant and business theorist, says of business managers, "there are only two kinds of managers, the quick and the dead!" I believe that phrase applies to all business people, regardless of vocation. To thrive in today's, fast-paced, chaotic environment one must seize the opportunity brought about by changing tastes and nutritional trends.

A farmer today must be prepared to re-examine every facet of production looking for areas of opportunity and saving. As land values increase and labor costs intensify, progressive farmers must be willing to explore the possibly of dispersed sites of production and less labor intensive methods.

For many years labor was viewed as a cost, and equipment was viewed as an investment. Wages, associated costs, and workers compensation are rising steadily. A shortage of labor is a trend that is predicted to continue. This trend intensifies the demand for well-trained, dedicated employees. Labor is a limiting factor in every agricultural business operation. In the past, you were expected to grow your commodity, sell through impersonal channels, and indulge in as little variation as possible. Today the market rewards variety, differentiation, and personal relationships with increased profits. The movement to sell agricultural goods at farmers' markets may presage what is happening throughout the agricultural industry.

The movement toward farmers' markets may exert various pressures on the food industry. First, a clean, wholesome, chemical-free food supply has become synonymous with these markets. The variety of fresh produce made available in open-air farmers' markets is inviting. In addition, farmers' markets allow the public direct contact with the grower. Customers are encouraged to get to know the person who is responsible for the food. That is a selling point the average American farmer today cannot trump. The experience of shopping at a farmers' market may be the drive behind other experiential opportunities for you to explore.

Commodity to Private Label

In the agricultural world of yesterday, commodities ruled. Today, there has been a significant change. Consumers are now willing to pay extra for unique and specialized products. Customers are seeking individual relationships with suppliers and vendors as never before. They want safe, healthy, and convenient food sold through a personal relationship of trust.

> **Case Study**
>
> Paul and Kathy decided it was time to expand from 400 acres in Northern California to 1100 acres in Southern Oregon. Thus, they jumped into a large farming operation in order to integrate the lamb market vertically. They went from being a small "mom and pop" lamb breeder

to a provider of lamb packaged for the restaurateur. Their vision was to provide wholesome, organic lamb to the finest restaurants on the west coast. They planned to provide lamb that they prepared from birth to box.

By adding a private label and developing a repu-tation for quality, the demand for their lamb should be strong. Their biggest concern as they project future business growth is keeping up with the demand as they navigate a fully integrated business model.

Developing a private label allows farmers to differentiate product and develop individual relationships with customers. I use the expression "box it" to describe a business system that is uniquely yours. If you cannot put it in a box, you do not own it. In every business endeavor—be it an almond farm in northern California, an irrigation design company in Oregon, or a produce company in Arizona—each has a unique system or characteristic that distinguishes its operation.

Agribusinesses may look very much the same. They may be sized according to some universal measure. They may use very similar inputs of production. They certainly produce to a very large extent a very homogeneous product (commodities). The implication is of sameness.

Putting your business operation in a figurative box will help you to find the uniqueness in your product, service, or operation. That uniqueness may be as simple as a more efficient cultivation method. It may be more complex such as how you handle a particular product to ensure freshness after harvest. It may be a method of diversification such as growing produce specific for the local farmers market. "Box it," implies a proprietary process or product. It is "how it is done here." It is a unique characteristic of your operation designed to maximize the return of the business.

The foundation for a good business must be in place before you scatter your resources looking for a "quick fix." The preceding paragraphs are designed to give you some food for thought as you begin to design the business that will transition through the generations.

Case Study

I was recently talking with a farmer, Dave, who shared with me something so startling that I asked him to repeat what he said. "My newest employee has been with me for seven years. The other two have been with me for 27 and 32 years respectively." I heard it this time. I was amazed. Of course, it begged the question, How did you achieve this? Dave sat a little straighter noticing that I was sincerely impressed by his achievement. Dave said, "I treat them right. The wages may not sound like much, but when you add in the benefits, housing, family health plan, and retirement, you have a pretty good wage for the work." I asked why he paid so well, especially compared to the rest of the industry. His retort made perfect sense. As he spoke, I felt as if I were listening to a CEO of a major corporation. "Training costs money; it takes time, and turnover causes the farm to be too dependent on me. Keeping long-term employees who know their job well allows me the freedom to concentrate on high-value activities. If I have people who take responsibility in the business and become accountable for their results, I can do other things that make money for the business."

Dave is probably unaware of just how advanced his business thinking is. His farm operation is very progressive, especially considering its relatively small size. The proof of his progress, and a lesson from which every business person could benefit, is that labor is not necessarily a cost. When you factor in the benefits of long-term employees dedicated to business success, it is difficult to imagine them as an expense. Labor must be regarded as an investment. Like other systems on the farm, a skilled labor force improves the bottom line.

Your goal should be a thriving business, not one that just limps along. To achieve that, you need to focus on business transforming trends. It is important to emphasize to farmers and agribusiness owners that in today's world you do not have time to evolve your business.

The Department Of Agricultural Economics at Purdue University published "Farming in the 21st Century" on August 31, 1999. This article compares both old and new concepts.

Table 3:1	
Old Concepts	**New Concepts**
Commodities	Specific attribute/ differentiated raw material
Staple Products	Fashion/Niche products/ projects
Assets drive the business	Customer drives the business
Hard assets (land, machinery, buildings)	Soft assets (people, organization, plans)
Blending of commodity product from multiple sources	Separation of identity-preserved raw materials
Geographically concentrated production sites	Geographically dispersed/ separated production sites
Owning assets	Controlling assets
Labor is a cost/equipment an investment	Labor is an investment/ equipment is a cost
Sell product/give away service	Sell service/give away product
Impersonal/open markets	Personal/negotiated/closed markets
Impersonal sourcing and selling	Relationship sourcing and selling
Stability	Change/chaos/flexibility
Core Competencies	New/different/unique skills and capabilities
Tradition/remembering	New ideas/forgetting
Public/open information, research and development	Private/proprietary/closed information, research and development

chapter 4
COMPLETE BUSINESS PLAN

There is no right or wrong way to create a business plan. A business plan is not a panacea, but it does make a difference in the level of success of any given business. A well-executed business plan can make the difference between mediocrity and success, good and great, and great and world class. A well-written business plan provides instructions on how a business should be run. It also offers specific guidelines for decision-making and allows for changing conditions.

The rudiments of planning anything usually follow the same structure of a business plan. Initially, you identify specific goals or objectives derived directly from your vision. What do you want to accomplish? Your vision statement is followed by a thorough review and analysis in which readily available resources are examined, identifying what needs to be developed or acquired to realize an opportunity. What characteristics may impede the opportunities you are trying to exploit? Each goal or objective is supported by a specific action. The realization of the goal through focused activity derives the best results.

Progressive Business Planning

A business plan is an articulation of company goals and the action steps that need to be taken to realize these goals.

A business plan also includes information that supports the objectives of the company and may address the strategies for marketing products, managing personnel, and systems operation.

To survive through multiple generations, businesses must build and abide by a plan for success. That plan must be dynamic (i.e., tending toward change or productive activity; energetic; vigorous; or forceful), motivating, and progressive in nature. It must be flexible and vigorous enough to adjust to changing conditions, shifting resources, variations in consumption habits, regulative initiatives, and evolving abilities. A dynamic plan is a motivating factor for you, your family, and the employees in your business. People, whether employees, third-party vendors, strategic alliances, or family members, must be motivated. People enjoy being a part of a bigger plan, a part of a vision to grow something bigger than they could grow on their own. The bigger your vision, the better your plan, the more likely it will inspire others. Everyone wants to be a part of something that is progressive and dynamic. Forward motion, though difficult to sustain, is crucial in this fast-paced world...

- How can so-and-so outpace me this year?
- Does my competitor know something I do not?
- Does my business demonstrate a weakness just waiting to be exploited?

You must strive to develop and grow your business at every opportunity. Progress is exciting. It fuels the fires to work harder and keep a sharp eye out for opportunity. Though a business plan is reviewed and refined each year, it should be written with a long-term perspective.

A complete business plan addresses at a minimum the following topics:

1. Vision or mission statement
2. Company history and guiding values
3. Management responsibilities
4. System changes and improvements
5. Analysis of strengths, weaknesses, opportunities, and competition
6. Clearly defined goals and objectives
7. Action plans to support each goal
8. Budget to project income and expenses
9. Review and evaluation

STEP 1: VISION OR MISSION STATEMENT

A clear vision or a mission statement is where a business plan begins. It is a description of exactly how your business will look when you have achieved your objectives.

- What do you want to see when your business is built and your vision is realized?
- Is it running smoothly, and is it paying increasing profits?
- Can you describe what this "looks like" so that it can be shared with those people who are instrumental in helping you realize your vision?

For most, a vision statement may be easier said than done Your ability to articulate a vision statement clearly make the difference between a good business operation and a great one. A complete vision statement is the foundation of a business plan. The business plan is an instruction manual to help create your vision.

Imagine that you are driving to a place for the first time on a beautiful day. As you drive, you notice a beautiful farm off in the distance. The barns and outbuildings are painted the perfect shade of red. The white fences appear to be straight and in excellent condition. The fields are a lush emerald green. The home, barnyard and outbuildings are shaded by decades-old shade trees, the perfect place to stage any and all farm activities. You note with a tinge of envy the beautiful crops and the extreme level of care. No doubt you have seen this picture-perfect farm before. This is a point I refer to as the point of perfection.

The idea behind a point of perfection is that everyone has one. Our collective job, yours as proprietor and mine as coach, is to discover this point of perfection —wherever it may be. Define your point of perfection exactly. Set goals to reach it, and then implement the action steps required to bring it to fruition. Your business, be it a farm, ranch, or agribusiness, can have the same point of perfection. If you had all the necessary resources, could develop the talent, and could apply the ingenuity, how would your business appear? The description that you share and the words you write will help you to refine the perfect business model.

You can use an exercise similar to the personal vision statement completed in Chapter 1. However, only apply the direction specifically to your business interests, the farm, ranch, or agribusiness, rather than to your life as a whole. You may notice a significant overlap as it is nearly impossible for a true entrepreneur to define himself or herself in terms that do not in some way connect to a vocational interest.

A vision is a written statement of the basic intent or purpose of your farm/agribusiness. It is the mental image of how your business should look, feel, and perform. You should explore your vision from the perspective of owner, employer, and chief executive officer. The business should be viewed through the critical eyes of the customers that you serve and from the viewpoint of your employees as they work to bring your vision to fruition. Your vision statement should support your personal values and goals. It is the foundation for building an effective business plan. Consider the questions below as you write your vision statement.

- How do you want your farm/agribusiness to appear?
- In what products or services do you want to specialize?
- How do you want to be perceived by your customers?
- How do you want your employees to treat your customers?
- What should the physical appearance of your farm/equipment say about your operation?
- How much family involvement do you want in the business operation?
- Do your actions, the appearance of your plant and equipment, and the systems with which you manage the business operation support the values you want to promote?

Example: Vision Statement

Legacy Farms, FLP, will continue to take a leadership role in the cattle industry of Southwest Montana. It will continue to develop a specialized line of beef and proceed with the goal of integrating the processing facility. Our goal to vertically integrate our business model from the cow/calf operation to restaurant deliveries of boxed beef will drive our management and systems decisions in the coming years. We hope to become the dominant source of beef for the prime restaurant market in the Pacific Northwest.

1. Does the vision statement give you a clear understanding of the guiding goals and direction of Legacy Farms, FLP?

STEP 2: COMPANY HISTORY AND GUIDING VALUES

A brief company history, including guiding principles and values, is an additional piece of the foundation of a business plan. The company history provides background on its culture and philosophy. To get started, use statements such as:

- "What we've always done here..."
- "We always prevail because... "
- "If Granddad were here he'd say..."

History gives perspective. The "cultural memory" shared through a company history stabilizes the ship in the storms of change. It provides fortitude against the winds of challenge. Cultural memory establishes a safe haven from the day-to-day pressures of competition, legislative change, and economic cycles.

Many farm/agribusiness owners struggle with the question of guiding principles or values. However, a brief history of the company will allow you to discover what makes you unique. Guiding values and principles may be as simple as, "We demonstrate industry in everything we do." Simply using the word "industry" describes your industrious (diligent) nature. It defines the driving motivation that directs your business effort with 110% commitment. Most businesses like to be recognized as an honest or truthful. Most want to be seen as generously giving back to their industry, their community, or to charitable organizations. Whatever your guiding principles or values may be, you should include them in your business plan as a written statement of your philosophy.

Writing the company history for a family-owned business is similar to writing a family history. An interviewee, a proprietor of a very successful agribusiness, seemed to have many of the pieces in place for a successful succession and estate plan. On review, I realized that the biggest piece missing from his succession plan was a brief company history that contained an explanation of the values on which the business was built. Given that the owner repeatedly stated that he wanted the business to perpetuate and maintain his founding values, this part of the business plan was critically important. In fact, he felt motivated to insure a continuation of the business so that his values could live on after him.

- How was the business founded?
- Why was the business founded?
- What unique characteristics make this farm/ agribusiness different from all of the others?
- Name three strengths specifically exploited to an advantage in this operation.
- Name three weaknesses that were overcome to make the operation more profitable.

- If you were to change any part of the operation, what part of the operation is not subject to change under any circumstances?
- From the above questions can you list ten guiding principles or values?

Example: Company History and Guiding Values

Legacy Farms. FLP, is a leader in the prime cattle business serving the Pacific Northwest restaurant market. The company was founded in 1892 as a 160-acre homestead in Belgrade, Montana by my great-great-grandfather, Cyrus A. Spafford. The company has passed through four generations, survived the depression, and thrived during two world wars. The challenges of the beef industry, particularly cattle production, have been great, especially weathering the anti-red meat phenomenon of the late 1970s and 1980s. Through each and every challenge, we have survived through aggressive marketing and ruthless expense control. We have maintained a strong capital position throughout our company history to not only weather the storms of cyclical markets and fickle consumers but also to capitalize on opportunities to grow, diversify, and expand (especially when our competitors may be financially stretched.

Today we raise beef from birth to market. We grow feed for consumption and sale, and butcher/box/market directly to consumer restaurants in the northwest states of Washington, Oregon, Idaho, and Montana. Our history guides our future. We use long-established values to guide our decision-making process.

Family, extended family, and loyal employees are the strength of our workforce. Though family is important, a name does not guarantee a job. As either a direct family member or a descendent of a loyal employee, we realize that the depth of character of the individuals that comprise our workforce determined the depth of character of our company.

Our guiding principles are simple and concise. These values include industry, integrity, and quality. Industry means we work very hard to answer the challenges and maximize the opportunities of our business. Integrity speaks for itself. Quality is demonstrated in every facet of our business.

- Does the history of Legacy Farms, FLP, give you a clear sense of where it has been?
- Does the company history give you a strong sense of direction?
- Does it impart a sense of direction, growth, and development, based on sound principles?

STEP 3: MANAGEMENT RESPONSIBILITIES

A clear statement of management's strengths, responsibilities, and capabilities reinforces the vigor of a company. A company is said to be only as good as the people who work there. The vigor of a company is only as good as the leadership that drives the company. This section of the business plan is designed to give confidence to team members, support management/personnel decisions, and detail some of the critical responsibilities of the management team. This section of the plan details management development efforts. Management today is not a seat-of-your-pants vocation. Leaders need education and development to succeed in today's marketplace.

Development programs should be tailored to serve the individual needs of managers.

Just as a business plan details the systems, machinery, and tools necessary to vertically integrate a market, a business needs managers with the skills and abilities necessary to handle a planned new endeavor. Your business plan should detail the management needs of the operation based on company direction. It should also detail the development necessary to ensure that management is ready to succeed.

The depth of a sports team's bench often makes the difference in a game. Business is no different. The depth of your "management candidate bench" determines your ability to succeed. Too many businesses run short in this critical area. Personnel development is the biggest challenge facing a business owner. The opportunities to grow a business can be severely limited if you do not have the right personnel with the right skills at the right time. Conversely, with a bench full of good people ready, willing, and able to meet the challenge of a new venture, you may be surprised by the opportunities that knock at your door. In this section of the business plan, you may want to address the depth of management candidates and the training that can be given to develop the skills and abilities necessary to lead.

Writing the management responsibility section of the business plan forces you and your current management team to take a close look at the resources that are available to grow or to constrain growth. A synopsis of your management structure, accompanied by a brief statement of responsibility, establishes the current status of the business.

Though you share current goals in another section of the business plan, a summary of new ventures or developing business establishes a benchmark for management development. Where is the business headed based on consumer trends, industry demands, or underutilized resources? If the business is going to head in a new direction, what kind of management structure will serve the new enterprise?

- What is the current ability or educational and skill limitations of the management team?
- For which business functions or operational systems are our
  managers currently responsible?
- What kind of development is necessary to improve the skills and abilities of our current management team?
- What kinds of management skills and abilities are necessary to manage future business?
- What is the depth of our bench, and how can we improve the depth and breadth of our management team candidates?

Example: Management Responsibilities

The next phase of our expansion of Legacy Farms, FLP, requires an assistant manager for the processing plant, sales, department, and delivery. Since the cow-calf operation is our most tenured operating division, we will assess that department for management candidates. We currently have a combination of ten loyal employees and family members who comprise our management candidates. The officers and current management staff will meet with each of these candidates to assess his or her individual interest in assuming a role with increased responsibility. Then we will meet with each interested candidate to design a development plan to develop the skills and abilities necessary to help Legacy Farms, FLP, move into our prescribed vertical integration opportunities.

Table 4:1

Management Position	Management Responsibility	Development Focus
Katherine Shulman	President, majority owner	Currently attending classes in marketing and food science. New venture as a wholesaler to restaurants.
George Shulman	Vice President, owner, Cow-Calf Operation	Currently experimenting with local feed source to improve weight gains.
Peter Spafford	Vice President, owner, Wholesale Operation	Currently studying personnel issues for expansion and manufacturing to expand processing plant.

- Did you identify your areas of strength?
- Did you discuss your current structure and any changes in the coming year?

- Did you identify management needs and your source of candidates to address those needs?
- Did you identify development needs and a source or plan for development?

STEP 4: SYSTEM CHANGES AND IMPROVEMENTS

Increased efficiency or better economies of scale are required to realize any business growth, development, expansion, integration, or change. Increased efficiency or better economies of scale require a business to improve its operating, management, staffing, or processing systems. The ability to replicate systems is an important consideration as you decide to expand your business. Without the ability to replicate the systems of a successful operation, you must be available 24/7 to guide and direct each business activity. You become the micromanager or the operational speed bump in the path to business success. If, on the other hand, you can design your business as a system of activities that can be replicated, you allow yourself the freedom to expand. Most business activities are jobs or duties repeated on a regular basis. Most activities can be devised as a system of duties repeated over and over again to get a consistent result.

Efficiency dictates that you learn to systematize jobs. This effort pays off in an improved bottom line. That is because of increased efficiency and the ability to hire someone capable of repeating the same actions. As you explore the expansion of the most promising systems, those that can be eliminated are obvious.

With each new expansion comes the need to devise systems or a series of tasks to manage a job efficiently.

Systems allow you to troubleshoot a job that is not satisfactorily completed. Systems allow for delegation without immediate supervision.

When you write this section of the business plan, in practice you only address the system changes or improvements that occur during the effective dates of the business plan. As an ongoing business, most of your systems are in place and are reinforced in job descriptions, employee handbooks, and operating manuals. Covering systems changes and improvements in a business plan is designed to explain a change in current operation due to expansion, integration, development, or change.

- What specific changes are expected due to expansion, integration, development, or changes?
- Systems changes/improvements could be due to new equipment, facilities, or implements.
- Systems changes are usually a simplification based on improved efficiencies.
- New equipment can improve efficiencies beyond the immediate area the equipment is designed to address. A new piece of equipment may cause a ripple effect of system change.

Example: System Changes and Improvements

Peter Spafford, as Vice President of Wholesale Operations, will design an integration plan for the new processing equipment due in the first quarter of the new year. The meat processing operation will shut down for 21 days during the first quarter. During that time, Peter will supervise a through cleaning of the packing facility.

Any "deferred maintenance" will be dealt with as necessary to ensure that everything is in order for start-up following the installation of the new equipment.

According to recommendations of the manufacturer, Peter will design a new work schedule employing 11 workers over two shifts a day. The current operation employs 15 over three shifts a day. Once the new equipment is installed, training will commence with the assistance of the manufacture for one month following start-up. Between now and start-up, Peter will schedule the two shifts, decide who will fill the available positions (now 11 instead of 15), and then offer the extra four people to George to help with the Cow-Calf operation.

- Did you address a system improvement?
- Will it improve your operation, expand efficiency, and eliminate waste?
- Did you clearly address an area of improvement or development?

STEP 5: ANALYSIS OF STRENGTHS, WEAKNESSES, OPPORTUNITIES, AND COMPETITION

Analysis demands a critical eye and an objective point of view. Time and effort must be invested exploring what may be possible. What areas of opportunity exist related to your farming operation? A thorough analysis examines every aspect of your business. How can your operation be managed better, faster, stronger, or more profitably than in the past? Analysis measures your available resources. Given your business resources, the characteristics of your current operation and the market for various products, what can you change, adjust, or rededicate to increase profits, develop new markets, or diversify offerings?

A thorough analysis of your farm business takes into account strengths, weaknesses, opportunities, and competition. Analysis looks at external and internal features of your farm operation. Analysis provides a realistic basis to identify the best opportunities for you to grow. That will help you avoid wasting time and money. Consider the questions below as you complete your analysis.

Internal development opportunities
- What areas or opportunities exist for growth?
- What resources of your operation may be underutilized
- Can you design better systems for the management of operations?

External market opportunities
- What trends in the market are most prevalent?
- What segments of the population might you target?

Competitive review
- Who are your competitors?
- How and why do you exceed your competitors' value proposition?
- What experience can we provide for our customers that is not currently available in the marketplace?

Quality analysis (quality review – trend analysis)
- In which quality areas are you succeeding?
- In which areas is improvement needed?

Various farm advisory agencies can help you explore any area, including, product, pricing, demand, growth trends, consumer taste/fashion trends, and commodity production requirements or recommendations. A thorough analysis allows you to develop realistic goals and action plans for the growth of your business.

- What weaknesses and strengths can you identify?
- How do you best minimize a weakness while maximizing a particular strength?
- What are your farm's positive attributes?
- What opportunities do you see in the future based on fashions, trends, and tastes?

What segment of the farming operation or business management needs the most improvement? Who are your competitors? Do they present a challenge to be addressed or overcome?

Example: Analysis of Strengths, Weaknesses, Opportunities, and Competition

Strengths
   • Size, one of the largest cattle operations in Montana.
   • Vertically integrated, breeding to box, though new, we are secure in our market share.
   • Demand exceeds supply.
   • Positioned for continued growth.
   • Resources to support growth/development objectives.

Opportunities   • Demand exceeds supply.

- Economies of scale due to recent growth allow for improved bottom line without additional investment.
- Demand for organic beef/feed offer opportunity for growth.
- Consulting work may represent a new market.
- Offers to buy smaller producers, improve size economies.

Weaknesses
- Charting new territory. No business model to emulate.
- Management may be inexperienced in depth considering our recent vertical integration.
- Cost to market/delivery is increasing.
- Primary customers are in Western Washington.
- American diet adds to the cyclical nature of the business.

Competition
- Farmers with lesser quality beef can shave costs to consumer-priced competition.
- Foreign beef sources (Canada) can offer some price concessions.
- Pork and poultry markets offer cost-conscience consumer alternatives.
- National wholesalers can offer quantity discounts.

- Did you specifically address strengths, weaknesses, opportunities, and competition? If you specifically addressed strengths, weaknesses, opportunities, and competition, you can build a business plan that addresses each concern.

Does an exhaustive analysis allow for better management of the business? If you know where you are strong, you can use it to your advantage. If you know where you are weak, you know where not to compete. If you know where there is opportunity, you can exploit that opportunity. If you know the competition, you can devise a plan to surmount it.

STEP 6: CLEARLY DEFINED GOALS AND OBJECTIVES

Defining goals and objectives may be the most difficult part of the business plan. Goals and objectives become commitments. Everybody appreciates a commitment from someone else, yet no one wants to make one. One of the biggest fears, tantamount to a fear of heights, is the fear that you will be held accountable for your commitments. The only sure way to accomplish anything is with a clearly defined objective or goal.

Goals identified through your analysis will become priorities for the year. You should focus on areas of improvement in each area of your analysis, such as market, crop, infra-structure, or personnel development. Your goals represent steps to realize your vision. Like a razor-sharp arrow, the more focused your goals, the more likely you are to hit your target. Goals also provide a basis for measurement and evaluation of your planning effectiveness.

- What are your production goals?
- What new products or segments of the market will you target?
- What consumer trends/fashions will you address?

- How will you maximize the return on your production investment?
- How will you identify opportunities to improve a production input or procedure?
- What skills or abilities should respective managers or employees develop to meet company goals?
- What are your personal goals?

Example: Clearly Defined Goals and Objectives

We understand that specific goals and objectives committed to action are the life blood of a business plan. Legacy Farms, FLP, commits to several business goals in a year. We asked our management team to set individual department goals designed specifically to support the overall business goals. As a company in the New Year, we will accomplish the following:

1. Improve prime beef restaurant sales by 12.5%.
2. Complete the processing plant remodel and cut operating costs by 10%.
3. Purchase the Prather operation and begin to integrate organic beef and feed into our product line.
4. Select and begin the development process of a new management candidate for future growth or expansion in organic products or our sales department.
5. Research the validity of developing a proprietary beef product to enhance product line.

- As a company, did you detail specific goals for the year?
- Is there any doubt or discrepancy regarding the specificity of each goal?

- Did you limit goals to a reasonable number so that all concerned can concentrate efforts and succeed?
- Are your goals realistic yet motivating?
- Do your goals move the company toward the ultimate vision spelled out by leadership?

STEP 7: ACTION PLANS TO SUPPORT EACH GOAL

Constructive action supports a worthy goal. A detailed action plan must be designed to support each objective in your business plan. An action plan can be as simple as a to-do list or as complex as an instruction manual. Each goal, its situation, the resources available, and the expected working conditions dictate the level of detail necessary in a written action plan.

Action Plans are necessary to concentrate your limited resources, time, money, and production inputs, to the areas you plan to develop or grow. Determine what your action plans are to reach your goals. Each action plan is enumerated, including a time line and a person accountable for the action.

Answer the following for each goal:

- What steps are necessary to achieve each goal?
- What resources will be devoted to each goal?
- Who is responsible for achieving the goal?
- Who will assist in the execution of this activity?
- What is the time line for each activity related to this objective?
- What is the system for follow-up in relation to this objective?

Example: Action Plans to Support Each Goal			
Goal: Improve Prime Beef Restaurant sales by 12.5%.			
Step	Action	Assigned	Date
Survey current customers	One of the best ways to learn how to attract more customers is to survey your current customers. Discern what you do right, what you can do better, and how to serve better.	Katherine with clerical staff	01/05 thru 02/05
Attend northwest food shows	Food shows have always been an opportunity to meet current customers, reinforce relationships, and meet potential new customers. This year we plan to double our participation. We will attend six shows instead of three.	Management staff with appropriate employee assistance	01/05 thru 04/05
Sponsor cooking tutorial	Advertising today has become intrusive. Legacy Farms, FLP, will focus on attracting new customers by offering a complimentary cooking tutorial to help restaurant owners train and develop cooking staff.	Peter Spafford	01/05 thru 08/05
Personally contact potential customers	Follow-up immediately with potential customers from referrals, cooking tutorials, and food shows. If we regularly receive referrals from existing customers, our focus will be follow-up.	Entire staff, management, and support	01/05 thru 12/05

STEP 8: BUDGET TO PROJECT INCOME AND EXPENSES

Money is the fuel that fires the business engine. Your investment is dollars, sweat, tears, and time. Your return is income for the family, equity to pass to the next generation, and satisfaction that you have built something of lasting value. Motivation comes in many forms. Your direct reward comes in financial appreciation. Money provides measurable feedback that reinforces the value of your work.

A complete business plan is supported by an extensive budget. A budget is a detailed projection of income and expenses for a given project or business venture. The exercise of completing a budget validates the expected investment and the projected return of a given project or venture. At times, we act as if money is a secondary consideration for a project. A positive return on investment can be a motivating force for you and your management team.

A budget basically involves two components, expected financial investment and projected financial return. Some expenses are fixed, while others are variable. Some are long-term, such as a lease or mortgage payment. Others are short-term, such as a one-time payment or a contract paid over less than one year. Income is measured on an income/expense statement, profit and loss, or a simple sales invoice. Equity is measured on a balance sheet as net worth.

Like the other pieces of the business plan, the budget is not a "once done" proposition. It must be reviewed and refined throughout the course of the year. Every projection is continuously evaluated. If you project an amount, did the actual result cost more or less? Did a particular investment meet or exceed expectations? Management should always be concerned with why.

Why did our projections do better or worse than originally planned? Can we learn to make more accurate projections?

Your budget may include (but should not be limited to) the following topics:

1. Projected cash flow from operations is a detailed forecast of gross sales, cost of goods sold, gross profits, and expected fixed and variable expenses. This forecast can be applied to a spreadsheet and made to cover a number of years. If you can project your expected cash flow for the year you can plan around periods of greater expense or smaller income.

2. Projected net income includes net sales less costs of goods sold and expected fixed and variable expenses. This forecast is made on an annual basis and broken down by month.

3. Sales projected by month will help to track progress toward the goals in your business plan. Remember, nothing happens unless you sell something.

4. Cost of goods sold projected by month is a breakdown of the costs of production or the costs to sell units of production. It is a very good tool to measure expenses on a per sales basis.

This is only a partial list of the possible projections you can make through your budgeting exercise. The important point is a plan is only as good as the information you put into it. Financial projections can be time-consuming and tedious, yet the reward comes in a better managed business.

A budget starts with an estimate of the fixed and variable costs of running your agribusiness. A budget allows you to plan for production inputs during a given year. It will allow you to plan for the financial costs of changes, improvements, or development. Most years you will find the budget or the dollars spent actually follow a trend based on your production. Large variances come when you change or target a specific area for growth.

1. A budget should measure areas of concern.
2. A budget should focus on important financial considerations.
3. A budget should be accurate, reviewed, and updated on a regular basis.
4. A budget should always be compared to the actual results. Are you on budget, over budget, or under budget?

Example: Budget to Project Income and Expenses				
Category	2006	2007	2008	Assumptions
Sales				
Less cost of goods sold				
Gross profit				
Expenses				
Delivery				
Depreciation				
Donations				
Employee benefits				
Utility expenses				
Insurance				
Leasing expenses				

Legal and accounting				
Miscellaneous				
Office expenses				
Payroll taxes				
Repairs and maintenance				
Rent				
Wages				
Total expenses				
Net income				

1. Your projections should be clear and concise.
2. Your projections should be based on financial goals, your business plan, economic conditions, and reasonably justified estimates.
3. Your budgets should be reviewed continuously throughout the year. As conditions change, budgets are adjusted accordingly.
4. No decision should be made without financial consideration.

STEP 9: REVIEW AND EVALUATION

Regular and consistent review is critical to the success of your business plan. You should regularly analyze your business activity.

- Are you achieving the level of success you projected (planned)?
- If you are, can you do better?
- Were your projections too low? If not, why not?

With detailed action plans and budgets to support expenditures, it is usually easy to discover why an objective is not met. The action plan allows you to trace accountability for each action. It is either getting done or it is not. You can trace expenses. Are you spending too much so profits are not as high as they should be? Or are you not spending enough to support some of the goals you may have set, such as entering a new market or streamlining a production procedure? Without regular follow-up, a business plan becomes an exercise in futility.

Regular follow-up may mean weekly, but no less than monthly. Frequency of reviews affects directly the immediacy of corrective action. Regular staff meetings are suggested. Consider meeting with your management team on a weekly basis. Have each manager meet with his staff (or group of employees) as often as needed. During each staff meeting, review, revise, and refine each company goal. You can troubleshoot problems, adjust for expense overruns, and minimize wasted efforts. Conversely, you may be able to capture an opportunity, adjust to a changing market condition, or address a short-term demand. Review current events and troubleshoot disturbing trends. Communication is an important key to your business success.

Without follow-up, the business plan fails. Periodic reviews, weekly, monthly or quarterly, generate important feedback information.

POINTS TO REMEMBER

1. Return on investment is an important measure for any given business expense. Periodic reviews allow you to check your progress.
2. Design the method of measure that best fits your operation. Systems of measure will help you keep track of your progress?

3. The management team should agree in advance on a follow-up procedure.
4. Follow-up with an investment/return analysis that ensures you focus on your resources wisely.
- Did you plan a complete agenda?
- Did you cover what is important according to the business plan?
- Did you invite all staff to participate?
- Did you allow time to adjust the agenda as necessary?

Remember, consistent review is the key.

Example: Review and Evaluation

1. Introduce any invited guest.
2. Review your business plan objective.
3. Review progress toward company goals.
4. Discuss and decide on a plan of action for any objective that may be out of line.
5. Review financial results, trends and projections. Adjust projections according the current status and trends.
6. Review personnel issues, work flow, quality, quantity, and responsibility.
7. Review current management and personnel development plans.
8. Review business systems, trends, opportunities, and competition.
9. Invite accounting, legal, and financial professionals as necessary to lend vocational expertise.

part 2
PLANNING FOR
ownership succession

A comprehensive succession plan ensures the smooth transition of the ownership and management of your agribusiness for the next generation. In most agribusinesses, the ownership and management of the operation are transferred to the same individual. The manager you select is critical to the success of the operation. A succession plan must include a process for selecting the most capable successor. With judicious implementation of the plan, you improve the odds of success for your agribusiness. As an owner leaving the business, financial support may be tied to the continued success of the business, whether or not you rely on note payments, consulting fees, or payments for a non-compete agreement. Your spouse and heirs may also be dependent on the continued success of the business. A financial hardship may follow a business failure caused by your death or disability. Whether you plan to pass the business to a relative, a loyal employee, or an unrelated third party, having a trained management successor ready to assume control automatically makes the business more valuable.

chapter 5
APPROACHES TO OWNERSHIP/MANAGEMENT SUCCESSION

Simplified Approach to Ownership/Management Succession

STEP 1: IDENTIFY THE POTENTIAL CANDIDATES

The first step in an ownership/management succession plan is to identify all of the potential successor candidates. You may consider family members, loyal employees, or candidates from outside current family and business circles. You may also consider competitors and third parties who may be seeking a merger or diversification opportunity.

STEP 2: MEASURE THE CURRENT SKILL LEVEL OF EACH CANDIDATE

Management aptitude is a critical factor in the selection process. Each candidate should be evaluated in both objective and subjective measures of management/leadership competence. An assessment should be used to measure current strengths and other characteristics that may need development.

STEP 3: EVALUATE THE NEEDS OF YOUR BUSINESS

You must understand the needs of your business. Some of the management skills necessary today may be insignificant in the future. Conversely, unimportant factors today may become paramount tomorrow. Mechanical ability, though critical today, may be less important tomorrow. Yet, computer skills and the ability to adapt technologically may be deciding factors in the competitive environment of tomorrow. When you compare the needs of the business with the management skills of each candidate, you will begin to understand what combination of management skills is important.

STEP 4: IMPLEMENT A PERSONAL DEVELOPMENT PLAN FOR YOUR MANAGEMENT CANDIDATES

Measure the skills, abilities, and educational demands of the management position against the resume of each candidate. Design a personal development plan based on the demands of the business and the developmental needs of each candidate. Work closely with each management candidate to ensure competency as you make your selection. Time together and attention to detail will allow you to assess the candidate's progress and attitude for assuming the management role.

STEP 5: COMMUNICATE WITH FAMILY MEMBERS AND LOYAL EMPLOYEES

Support from your family and loyal employees is critical to the transition of power and the continued success of your farm. Communication is key to enlisting the support that is necessary from family, employees, vendors, third-party suppliers, and financiers.

STEP 6: FOLLOW-UP

Without consistent follow-up a plan is not likely to succeed. People learn and develop business acumen at different rates. A development plan for management, especially as it relates to changing management, must be monitored.

Options for Ownership/Management Succession

There are basically three options for transferring ownership/management to the next generation or subsequent owner: transition to a family member, a loyal employee, or a candidate from the outside.

Transition planning is best initiated early in the life of your business. Your ownership successor must have time to learn the role of a leader. He must demonstrate leadership skills to existing employees, customers, and third-party vendors. The successor must show that he is prepared to lead the business effectively. With adequate time and a well-developed plan, a new owner can develop credibility. A gradual assumption of responsibility helps all parties to adapt to the transition. With a gradual assumption of duties, the new management person, customers, employees, and third-party vendors gradually acclimate to changing roles.

As with most decisions in life, you always have a choice. You can leave your business to a new owner voluntarily as part of a well-designed plan, or you can wait until you (or your heirs) are forced to act because of death, disability, or retirement.. A comprehensive succession plan covers both options. Most people want to control the timing and the conditions of the transition. Most people want to design a plan and include a default strategy for unforeseen circumstances. If your anticipated successor is still a child, you must plan for an interim manager to fill the leadership role until your child is ready.

TRANSITION TO A FAMILY MEMBER

Transition of ownership/management to a family member following retirement, disability, or death is not an uncommon scenario. If the trigger is your planned retirement, your role may change from owner to coach and then finally to note holder. Your continued involvement can add stability to the business operation.

TRANSITION TO A LOYAL EMPLOYEE

Leaving the farm to a loyal employee may be appropriate if you do not have children or if your children are not interested in the business. You may also ask a current employee to manage your business operation until your children reach a particular age or level of experience.

TRANSITION TO A CANDIDATE FROM THE OUTSIDE

You may decide to leave your agribusiness to a successor completely new to your business or to a third-party seeking to expand or vertically integrate their current business model. This may be appropriate if no one in your family is interested in assuming a leadership role.

Ensuring Equitable Distributions

Dividing the ownership of your agribusiness equally among multiple heirs is usually a recipe for disaster. Management by consensus is an inefficient way to run a business. The pitfalls of equal distribution can range from simple aggravation to devastating levels of discontent. By nature, "active" and "passive" owners have completely different objectives for business interests. Subsidiary operations or diversified business models divide business interests and authority where equal distribution is a concern. Many farmers look for expansion opportunities when they have more than one child who is active in the farm. In the case of passive heirs (children not working on the farm), owners often use other assets to equalize asset distributions.

The overlap between business interests and family relationships can be a major cause of emotional strain. As in other family situations, rivalries come into play. Emotional baggage is carried into each interaction and feelings of competition and inequity seem to surface. Acting impartially in choosing a successor may be next to impossible for a parent. The parent's allegiances must be divided among what is good for the family, the business, and themselves.

OUTSIDE ADVISORS

The issues of fairness, continued business success, and family harmony may be addressed by using an outside advisor to guide the succession planning and implementation process. Professional insight is the single biggest advantage to using an outside advisor. The advisor brings objectivity, experience, and education to the succession planning process. Succession planning is a once-in-a-lifetime event. The professional advisor will apply his multitude of experiences to help you. It is apt to be very difficult to separate emotional ties from the succession plan to make an impartial decision. An outside advisor is able to hold up the mirror of objectivity and is well positioned to do what may be impossible for you to do for yourself. An "unwritten code of fairness" may prevent you from communicating all of the necessary messages.

ROADBLOCKS TO SELECTING A SUCCESSOR

Choosing among your children is the single biggest roadblock to selecting a successor. This is especially true when multiple family members are involved in the farming operation. It may be that only one child works in the business, but he does not have the requisite skills to manage the operation. You may have several children but not all of them work in the business. You want to give them equal interests in the business ownership. What about your loyal employees? What if he or she is the right arm of your business? Loyal employees are the gold standard of a successful business. Now you must choose a child as successor in spite of the allegiance of that employee. The emotional strings that may be tied to this decision are not simple. You risk hurting a loved one and alienating a friend.

The sentiment tied to this decision may cause you to make an emotional choice rather than a business choice. Reluctance, as paralyzing as sentiment, exemplifies your unwillingness to let go. Letting go is second only to choosing one child over the other. You have spent your adult life in charge, controlling the many factors of the farm business. It is easy to talk in theory of changing control. Reality is much more difficult. Your reluctance about making a succession decision may result in losing a successor who applies his ambitions to another interest.

Comprehensive succession planning and implementing your exit strategy are not for the faint-hearted. You must be committed to the business needs of your farming operation, the harmony of family, and your own self-satisfaction. You must know that you have done your best to satisfy your obligation to these three important and interconnected, but separate, entities.

The best transition for you and your successor is a gradual transfer of responsibility. Concede your hesitation to let go. Use a realistic timeline for the transition process. Allow plenty of time for hands-on training. Give yourself time to pursue other ventures as you engage in a plan of gradual transition.

ENSURING A SMOOTH TRANSITION

A clear ownership/management succession strategy ensures a smooth, timely transition. Some points to consider:

1. Select a management successor well before your target transition date. Be it retirement, another venture in your vocational life, or some unforeseen crisis; time allows for the gradual assumption of responsibility and authority by your successor.

2. Communicate your succession strategy. Plan your method of communication to your supporting cast of family members, employees, customers, and third-party vendors. Communication is one of the most critical components of the comprehensive succession planning process. You must plan for communication opportunities.

3. Implement a management-training program. On-the-job experience is an important component of management development. On the other hand, supporting that experience with formal training programs, education, and mentoring relationships can lay a solid foundation for a budding owner/manager. Allowing other industry leaders to influence your choice of a successor through experiential learning may be a "jump-start" in the leadership process.

INVENTORY OF MANAGEMENT SKILLS

Competence assessments are nothing new in the corporate world. An assessment allows for an objective view of a potential leader's abilities. The skills and abilities assessed should reflect the needs of the business.

The traits of a good business leader are no different from those that most parents instill in their children. The role of a business leader may require more depth than other vocations. The traits of a good leader are competence, long-term commitment, personal integrity, and interpersonal communication skills. In addition to these character traits and an attitude of "growing toward excell-ence," a leader must also possess the ability to lead.

LEADERSHIP COMPETENCY

The ability to lead a business venture is the ability to envision the future, articulate the vision, and then muster the necessary resources, people, and production inputs to bring the vision to life. Leadership is difficult to define, but easy to recognize.

LONG-TERM COMMITMENT

The anomaly of business today is that it requires a long-term view, but quick solutions. Not every aspect of business is fun or exciting. In fact, some aspects are downright mundane, unpleasant, and stressful. A business leader must have a long-term view to weather the vicissitudes of business life. He must be able to see through the pains of today to reach the rewards of tomorrow.

PERSONAL INTEGRITY

Personal integrity requires an understanding of self. A person must be aware of the strengths and the char-acteristics in need of development. Does he or she recognize both and know how to work toward maximizing strengths while developing lesser skills?

INTERPERSONAL COMMUNICATION SKILLS

There is no substitute for the ability to communicate effectively. A leader must rely on communication skills to articulate a vision. He must consistently communicate to elicit support, borrow money, sell customers, and develop employees.

INVENTORY OF LEADERSHIP SKILLS

An inventory of leadership skills helps you to assess the skills and abilities of the succession candidates. The skills you observe in each candidate accompanied by a description of the depth and the breadth of each skill should be compared to the needs of the business.

Table 5:1. Leadership Skills Inventory			
Management Skills	**Level 1-5**	**Leadership Skills**	**Level 1-5**
Recognizes potential problems and attempts to troubleshoot.		Promotes a team spirit.	
Develops good safety habits, and demonstrates such.		Promotes a positive working environment.	
Performs well at all duties and responsibilities.		Recognizes potential areas of conflict and initiates mitigation.	
Exhibits patience and clarity in training others.		Understands quality and demonstrates a dedication to such.	
Completes outside training to improve job skills.		Performs as an integral part of a team.	
Demonstrates good computer utilization.		Demonstrates good business etiquette with customers and others.	
Uses good business systems/processes.		Uses good people development skills.	

Understands a business plan and can implement it accordingly.		Maintains confidentiality when appropriate.	
Uses excellent financial management skills.		Acts objectively in employee interactions.	
Can plan and budget for business growth and development.		Delegates with clear responsibility, and holds others accountable.	
Innovates to improve business systems/processes.		Mentors others in leadership development.	
Understands a particular industry.		Works as if success depends on his actions.	
Judiciously uses limited resources.		Develops good relationships with employees, customers, and others.	

MEASURING THE CANDIDATES' SKILL LEVEL

As you identify the business operations and leadership skills of each candidate, an assessment should be made about the depth of each skill. Your assessment should be objective. A relative number is assigned to each skill for each candidate. The number serves a dual purpose. First, it allows for a comparison among candidates. Second, this number establishes a base from which to judge the effectiveness of development plans and training programs.

The relative measure used must fairly reflect each candidate's skill. Skill evaluation for each candidate should be made by the same person or at the very least, using the same criteria. Business decisions, such as who will become the next owner/manager and what conditions have to be met before the final transition, will be made using this information. Given the candidate's development needs, how long until full responsibility is granted to the new management successor?

The completed assessment becomes the cornerstone of the candidate's development program. The candidate should be put in positions in which he or she can demonstrate strengths. Development programs are designed to improve business operations and leadership skills. Your goal through this entire process is as a well-balanced leader who can continue to develop your agribusiness.

CONSIDER THE NEEDS OF THE FARM OPERATION

Using the business plan, recall the vision you are trying to create. Certain features of your business need special attention. What are those features? Can you find a manager who has the skills necessary to develop the business? For example, the business plan calls for the development of a completely automated irrigation system, necessitating very strong computer skills. This is a three-year project that will completely transform the farm operation. One focus of your evaluation must be on the computer skills of the successor candidates you are considering. Do they have the requisite skills to implement the plan, completely integrate the irrigation system, and exploit the new efficiencies? Or should the successor candidate seek outside assistance, supplementing skill deficiencies by hiring a person with expertise in computers? Can the skills necessary to fulfill the job be learned through a development plan? The key is to match the strengths of the candidate with the requirements of the job. A manager's strengths will become the strengths of the business. Conversely, a manager's weaknesses will become the weaknesses of the business, that is, unless the manager candidate can overcomes those weaknesses.

chapter 6
DESIGNING A DEVELOPMENT PLAN FOR THE CANDIDATE

After you have identified the management candidates, assess their skills and measure their abilities. Share your business philosophy, ethics, and vision at the outset, and observe their work habits and interactions with other employees, customers, and vendors. The needs of the business as defined in the business plan will focus your attention on certain skills. Now build a development plan for each candidate, a plan that prescribes methods for improving the necessary management skills. The development plan is a detailed action agreement in which the candidate is held accountable for improving skills and abilities. Monitor progress regularly.

Development Plans for Owner/Manager Candidates

A development plan is an important component in the selection process for a manager. A development plan is an action plan that formalizes the training and development process between you and the candidate. It puts in writing what you ask a candidate to do to prepare for a bigger role in the family farming operation. Each plan is individualized for each candidate. The specific demands of your business are unlike any other. You may be in the same industry, grow the same commodity, and even sell to the same customers, but you do not farm the same land or have the same access to water, fertilizer, or equipment. You do not work with the same labor force, nor do you control the weather. Most importantly, your agribusiness is a combination of your vision and the foundation set by those who came before you. Your farming operation is a unique blend of people, geography, history, circumstances, and conditions.

Table 6-1. Owner/Manager Development Plan				
Skill/Ability	**Specific Action**	**Who**	**Date**	**Level 1-5**
Communications	Attend Butte College for Writing for Business workshop	Instructor	09/15-09/18	
Computer literacy	Attend Butte College for Computers in Farming class	Instructor	08/23-12/17	
Farm safety	Attend Farm Safety Workshop sponsored by Chico Farm and Supply	Instructor	02/01-02/03	
Business planning/vision	Work with current owners through the planning process for the coming year	Tom and Steve	10/01-01/31	
People skills/ teamwork	Assume responsibility for harvest crew. Work closely with Alfredo and the other team managers	Alfredo and others	07/15-09/30	
Business accounting	Work with family/business accountant. Learn bookkeeping, reporting, and budgeting	Accounting Company and associates	01/02-06/30	

Crop rotation	Assist in plan for next year's crop cycle	Tom and Steve	10/01-11/30	
Disease control	Attend agricultural extension workshop on disease control, and work with advisor for our farm concerns	Instructor and advisor	02/15-02/28	
Water management	Attend water board meeting with Tom. Assess concerns of coming year, and plan accordingly	Water board and Tom	Monthly	

A variety of methods should be used for the teaching and development of a new leader. Among the methods you may consider:

1. Demand outside work experience
2. Link to a mentor
3. Allow for on-the-job experience
4. Participate in classroom training at local colleges, industry seminars, and workshops
5. Attend business planning and strategy sessions with leadership team accountants and bankers
6. Attend commodity, coop, association, or grower meetings
7. Attend personal or group meetings with advisors and subject matter experts
8. Attend local farm bureau, farm alliance, or other political farm support group meetings

Some family business management experts contend that a good method for a young successor to gain experience is to work for another company. It is usually an excellent experience. The candidate gains another business perspective. It is a chance to observe various business management and leadership skills and learn other business systems. The candidate is not given special treatment, which is often given to family members. Achievement is based on merit alone.

WHEN THE SUCCESSOR OWNER IS A FAMILY MEMBER

Upon completing the candidate assessments, there should be enough information to begin to narrow your candidate pool. The process begins by pulling out the less able candidates in order to devote more time to better candidates. At this point, each candidate is working on a formal development program subject to your oversight and observation. In most cases, at least one of the candidates is a family member as the primary purpose of comprehensive succession planning is leaving your agribusiness to the next generation.

If you have a number of children in the business, the outcome of your selection process can bring mixed results. For instance, if one of your children is more qualified than his siblings and demonstrates the competence, dedication, and work ethic to become a successful manager of your agribusiness, you may face multiple issues with your less qualified children. Business dynamics will change, especially the relationship between the child you selected and the children you did not. If multiple children are equally qualified to run the business, you may want to consider multiple managers, subsidiary operations, expansion, or some form of specialization.

If you have only one child, and that person is interested and qualified to run the family farming operation, your focus changes from one of selection to one of preparation. Your goal becomes a gradual transition to a new manager with your guidance.

If there is no family member qualified or interested in running the family farm, you may consider outside sources, loyal employees, or maybe a sale.

YOUR CHILD'S SKILLS AND COMPETENCIES

It is almost impossible for a parent to be objective when assessing the skills, abilities, and competencies of a child. Many farm owners have a difficult time recognizing that their children do not possess the management competencies to become an owner/manager. At times, it may be equally difficult for a parent to admit that a child is ready to assume more responsibility. From a parent's perspective, children are always imagined as young and inexperienced.

One 65-year-old farmer with whom I talked had not yet assumed all of the duties of managing the family farm. His 91-year-old father refused to relinquish control. "You know, to your dad you are always nine years old," he said. Either way, an objective assessment can help you measure necessary skills and build an action plan to support development. The assessment can also be shared as a valuable tool with outside advisors who can look at each child objectively.

MULTIPLE QUALIFIED CHILDREN

Sibling rivalry is a normal part of family life. Fair competition among brothers and sisters is okay as long as the result is not war. When the dust settles and the successor is selected, you and your children must be able to go back to work as a productive team. However, it is to be expected that those children who were not selected may feel slighted. They may feel that they could do a better job. It is important at this point to resist the temptation to divide the management responsibilities equally among your children in an effort to minimize conflict. You may fear losing valuable talent or worse yet alienating one or more of your children. Before you divide management among multiple children in the name of equality, keep in mind that committees often have two speeds: slow and slower. The rivalry you were trying to avoid will now plague the business indefinitely. Rather than one leader you have now created an environment of power struggles, rivalry, and constant tension—none of which promote a successful work environment.

In an ideal world, your ownership structure would accommodate each child. Each child would be responsible for a subsidiary of the whole farming operation. With this structure, you individually recognize each person's contribution. However, most farm/agribusiness operations are not large enough to accommodate such an elaborate structure. Even if you could build a perfect structure, you would still need one person with the leadership abilities to pull all of the subsidiaries together.

It is doubtful that multiple managers could agree on every decision. With three managers, there is always the possibility that one person will be isolated from the group. Four managers could easily form two opposing teams. Leadership is critical and your job as leader is to set an example. Ideally, appoint an owner/manager with the leadership skills who can bring all of your children together, working toward a common goal.

EQUAL SHARES TO ACTIVE AND PASSIVE CHILDREN

If you have three children but only one wants to work the farm, you must determine how to treat everyone equitably by giving each party equal shares of assets (not equal shares of business ownership) to avoid sibling rivalries. As a parent, your emotional goal may be to state unequivocally that you want to treat all of your children fairly. Your may wish to divide ownership evenly, but doing so may have disastrous results. You will trigger a family conflict that could potentially affect everything you hold dear.

Rare is the farm/agribusiness in which all of the children in the family want to be involved in the business. Your children may want to pursue their own dreams, follow a spouse to another state, or raise a family under different circumstances. For simplicity, children working in the business are referred to as active and those working outside the family business as passive.

The biggest difference between your active and passive children is their goals. Yet, nothing more surely divides a family, negatively affects the business, and damages the individuals involved than pitting your active children against your passive children in a management tug-of-war. Active children want to develop the business. Development of the farm for themselves and future generations is their primary focus. Money earned is plowed right back into the farm to improve a given system, expand or diversify the products grown, or to improve some aspect of the current operation.

Passive children want income. From their standpoint, they have a large asset on the balance sheet, from which they expect to realize a nominal or fair rate of return. Unfortunately, farms do not work that way. In fact, passive children often have a large asset that returns very little, if anything. Perhaps the only pleasures these children can derive from the farm property are hunting privileges and bragging rights about owning a farm. The asset, by virtue of multiple ownership and non-controlling interests, has no marketable value. It cannot be sold. If the farm is passed to another generation, the current and future passive children will never realize anything other than a virtual interest in an illusional asset. "I own it, it looks good from the outside looking in, but in reality it is very much the same as nothing!" said one disgruntled passive partner. The common explanation for this outcome is equality. You may feel, "If I divide everything equally, isn't that fair?" My response is no; in fact, just the opposite is true. Furthermore, the active children are in a position which requires them to answer to the passive children for management decisions. The passive children feel they have a right to protect their interests in the family farm by participating in management decisions.

Your goal should be one of equitable transfers rather than equal division. 'Equal' implies each one of your children gets an identical share. Equitable is synonymous with fair. Equitable transfers are fair in that each child is offered a proportionate share of family wealth, which may not represent an equal ownership of the family farm/ agribusiness.

Setting Equitable Transfer Goals

Parents usually pride themselves on fairness and they attempt to treat each child equally throughout their life. If one child gets a new car, a trip for graduation, or a new hunting rifle, parents make sure to treat the other children the same. When a child gets married, parents often help with a down payment for the first home; they then try to do the same for the other children. Unfortunately, with an asset as large and as obligatory as your farm, dividing ownership equally among your children may be the blasting-cap for the dynamite keg that blows up many family businesses. Ownership divided equally among all your children, active and passive, is not fair to anyone. Active and passive children have two completely separate goals for their business interests and investment assets.

> ### Case Study
>
> Martha Coleman has been managing the farm since her husband died seven years ago. Though times have been tough, she wanted the operation to survive until her three sons were old enough to assume the management responsibility. Only her youngest son, Kyle is interested in farming. Indeed, he has been an exemplary asset to the business since his graduation from Montana State University three years ago. Jared Coleman is currently studying law at Northwestern and Zach Coleman has established himself as a residential contractor in the area. Martha's goal is to treat each child equally. She prides herself on how fair she is. Martha Coleman's simplified state:
>
> | | |
> |---|---|
> | Cash | $250,000 |
> | Farm/farm related assets | $2,500,000 |

Investment assets	$725,000
Total Assets	**$2,975,000**

Martha Coleman has two basic choices. She can divide her estate equally, leaving each son one-third interest in her total assets. Setting up a situation like this pits two passive owners against one active owner. Alternatively, she can leave the farm to Kyle as he is the only active child, and split the other assets between Jared and Zach Coleman. Though a better solution for family harmony, I am not sure that Jared and Zach would agree that the outcome is fair. Under the second solution, Jared and Zach end up with $ 487,500, while Kyle Coleman ends up with the farm and other farm-related assets worth $2,500,000.

A problem like this illustrates the enormity of the task at hand, including the financial constraints, the needs of the business for continued growth, and timing considerations for the ownership transition. The problem covers the emotions of each person involved, including spouses and extended family. These issues all play a role in the decisions made. Note too that this example did not even include the constraints imposed by estate taxes and inheritance obligations nor other financial obligations or retirement plans.

COMPETING GOALS OF ACTIVE AND PASSIVE CHILDREN

Conflict, sibling rivalry, and petty jealousy do not begin to describe the potential relationship-ending strain caused by dividing business assets equally among all of your children. Active children put the interests of the business first. They plow earnings back into the farming operation to enhance business development, diversify, expand, or replace aging equipment. Passive children want income or a tangible return on the value of the business as carried on their balance sheet. A passive owner can stonewall an active child's decision-making ability. The interference may be as simple as quibbling over minor business decisions and as serious as lost opportunities.

You say, "Okay I see your point; I will give full control to my active children. The passive owners will become 'stockholders in a corporation'. Problem solved!" I say no. The problem is just beginning. You, again, have given an asset that, to the passive child, has no value. Even a stockholder gets a vote, but most importantly stocks return dividends over time and, as a liquid asset, can be readily converted to cash. A non-controlling interest in a family business is not like owning shares of stock in a corporation.

Spouses and grandchildren exert a significant influence in the decision-making process. The dynamics created and the protective instincts awakened when spouses and grandchildren are a part of the picture, will alter all relationships. Spouses must be considered throughout the planning and implementation process. They can be a smoothing influence. They can become an ally of the business as co-manager, employee, support staff, or confidante. The opposite is also true. They can become an adversary in an attempt to protect their family from a perceived inequity. These feelings of protection and support are exaggerated when children are involved, especially if their own children (your grandchildren) express an interest in farming. In this case, preservation of the business for another generation becomes paramount. You begin to realize that your goals, and the objectives of your children, are virtually the same; to maximize your legacy for future generations of your family.

It is said that "timing is everything." For best practices, you must build a timeline into your transition plan. The specific timing is your call. The conviction you generate from your successors will be the result of excellent communication, sound reasoning, and a consistent transfer of responsibility and authority. A seed of resentment may be planted as ownership/management transition occurs with your active children while no assets or money are transferred to your passive heirs until death. Passive children must understand that your money and other assets will be used to fund the next venture in your vocational life or retirement. The money will not be squandered nor will it be given away. There is a difference between a business entity and wealth-accumulating assets. The success or failure of your succession plan, as it relates to the human element—feelings, understanding, or inequities—will be based on your communication. You must constantly remind your children, in-laws, and grandchildren what you are trying to accomplish:

1. "My goal is _____."
2. "Here is how I will accomplish that goal."
3. "This is the area in which I will need your help."
4. "This decision is for me to make, but I certainly appreciate your input."

FAIR DOES NOT MEAN EQUAL

To be evenhanded does not imply equal distribution. Your goal should be an equitable but not equal division. There is no way to divide your assets uniformly when a majority of your wealth is tied to a farm that is not going to be sold, but rather passed to subsequent generations as your legacy. Equal division of ownership, even with the best of intentions, creates tension, indecision, or destruction of your family unity. Active children must be given the opportunity to develop the family farm, free of interference from passive owners. Passive heirs must understand that some form of the family legacy is passed to them as well. Though tension cannot be avoided, it can be understood. If understood, it can be reasoned through to an amiable end for you, your business, and your family. You must strive for equitability rather than equality in your ownership transition plan.

As you establish a base for an equitable distribution of ownership, consider the personal contribution of each child involved in the farming operation such as:

- Sweat equity
- Indirect monetary loss of lost opportunities
- Minimal wages due to the familial nature of the business

It is important to determine the value of each active child's non-monetary contributions. Older children may contribute more due to strength, experience, or tenure. While some values, such as commitment and dedication, are hard to value, you are judge and jury in dividing ownership interests among your active children. The most important considerations are:

1. Is it fair to all concerned?
2. Was your justification well communicated?
3. Does everyone understand?
4. Did you use sound rationale?

Age is a factor in contributions made by your children. Older children typically assume more responsibility than younger children. Remember, children grow up fast. Do not overlook any child even though, as a teen, he or she may not be demonstrating a burning desire to follow in your footsteps. Make the young children aware of the possibilities. Help them to grow into contributing members of the business team, if there is any interest. Do the same for grown children who may be pursuing a career off the farm. As you consider leaving the ownership to the next generation, ask what level of involvement each child may want.

There is a big movement afoot today wherein families are returning to their roots. Your sons or daughters may want an opportunity to do this but do not know how to ask. Your hesitation to offer them that opportunity may seem prudent if you do not want to interfere. However, with everything to gain and nothing to lose, you definitely should broach the subject. Make your sons or daughters aware of the possibilities. You might be surprised by their reactions. Allow them the opportunity to vie for an ownership position. Then put a plan in place to develop the family farm for future generations.

Family history or poor communication skills may cause you to hesitate. If so, consider asking a professional advisor to intercede on your behalf. Ask the advisor to talk to your children about their interest in participating in the family agribusiness. Using an advisor lessens the potential for hurt feelings. For one reason, inquiring about your children's career choices may be a sensitive topic.

Using the skills of a professional allows for an objective conversation in an effort to include all of your children, both active and passive. Your children very well may open up to a professional, even though they are not comfortable to express their wishes candidly to you. This conversation may reveal a passion that will take your agribusiness to new frontiers.

As you examine the many facets of your succession plan, it is important that you remain multidimensional. Begin with a management transition plan, which will identify who may best develop the family farm for future generations. Communication throughout the process ensures family cohesiveness and understanding. The entire family must work together to realize the benefits of your legacy efforts. Each person must understand that all actions directly impact the outcome of the succession plan.

CHILDREN AS OWNER/MANAGER SUCCESSORS

Equality is the critical factor in discussing transfers to your children. The following issues summarize some very common owner/manager succession concerns:

- Is your retirement funded so that you may transfer the business ownership free of encumbrances? Will you require some form of retained ownership to fund your retirement or the next venture in your vocational life?

- Today is not too soon to begin the transition process. Considering your financial needs, the financial support for your spouse in case of unforeseen death or disability, and the income and capital needs of your successor, how much capital must be available?

- Have you communicated your intentions, clarified your goals, and addressed the concerns to all of your children? Have you carefully considered an ownership model designed to propel the family agribusiness to new levels of success?

- Have you adequately designed a manager development plan to address the needs of the business considering the current skills and abilities of each candidate?

- If your children are not old enough to assume management roles, will you consider an interim manager? If contemplating an interim manager, have you considered establishing a mentor relationship between your successor and your interim manager?

- Have you taken the time to develop working relationships with each son or daughter and their spouses? Are you satisfied with the relationships between your children and their spouses?

- Do your passive children express comfort with not receiving an equitable share of wealth until after your death? Jealousy and resentment may undermine family unity.

CHILDREN ARE EITHER ALL ACTIVE OR ALL PASSIVE PARTICIPANTS

If all of your children are active or all of your children are passive, equal distribution of ownership interests may make sense. When all of your children are active, you may consider transferring equal ownership shares to each child. The big decision in this case is– who will ultimately manage the business operation? Can you devise a management plan that includes each child exercising his or her strongest characteristics?

If all of your children are passive, an alternative for ownership may be as simple as equally divided shares, like stockholders in a corporation. Management is then shifted to an outside source such as an interested relative, a loyal employee, or a hired manager. If you sell your operation to someone outside your immediate family, you will then want to plan your estate, retirement, and investment alternatives accordingly. While selling a farm outright is the easiest and most equitable solution, it is less satisfying, considering that nearly everyone longs to leave a lasting legacy.

EQUITABLE DISTRIBUTIONS TO PASSIVE CHILDREN

Your plan should include a transfer of business assets only to your active children. Passive children should receive other assets outside the business. Equitable, or fair, distribution of your estate among active and passive children is important. When your plan is to distribute ownership interests only to active children, your passive children may become resentful. Specifically targeting non-farm assets to provide equitable transfers to passive children is a solution. Having most wealth tied up in farm assets is a dilemma most farmers face. Non-farm assets usually comprise a small percentage of the total assets on the farm owner's balance sheet.

NON-FARM / AGRIBUSINESS ASSETS

Substantial assets outside the business present another option. You may transfer the non-business assets to your passive children and the farm assets to your active children. The big issue when considering this type of arrangement is: when. Transferring the business during your lifetime promotes stability.

The business benefits, the family benefits, and you benefit.

Transferring non-business assets—cash, land, and equities—to your passive children should not happen until the settlement of your estate. Non-business assets may be utilized to fund your retirement or the next venture in your vocational life. Remember to focus first on your objective.

- What do you want to accomplish?
- Next focus on timing. When is the best time to give ownership to the next generation? And then, what is the best method, terms, and conditions to implement the transition? Always remember you have a choice regarding timing, terms, conditions, and methodology.

USING LIFE INSURANCE

Life insurance may help as you weigh the equitability of transfers among active and passive children. A well-placed life insurance program may benefit your heirs. Though very simplistic, and somewhat obvious, life insurance proceeds may allow your active children to receive the farm free of encumbrances and outside interference. Life insurance supplants the value of your business assets, passing equitable wealth to your passive children. Life insurance promotes evenhandedness offering all your heirs an equitable legacy. It allows peace of mind, and most importantly, it gives you the ability to maximize your legacy.

Life insurance benefits enhance your succession plans in two ways.

1. First, your passive children receive the proceeds from a life insurance policy as part of the settlement of your estate. The money that passes to your beneficiaries may be equivalent to the value of the business interests passed to your active children.
2. Second, the beneficiaries could be your active children. In this case, benefits will be sufficient to purchase the passive children's interest in the business; that is, if you allow the business to be equally divided, during your lifetime, to maintain family unity. You formalize this type of arrangement with a buy/sell agreement.

In most cases, passive children wait until your estate is settled in order to receive an inheritance. Life insurance does not change timing; rather it affects the certainty that money is available when a settlement, or buyout, is warranted. Life insurance offers freedom from concern as you invest in the next venture in your vocational life or as you seek retirement. You may spend your hard-earned money more freely, knowing that dollars are available to provide the legacy you desire. Once you know that you have control of the situation, you will feel much more relaxed. And, as the current ad proclaims, that is 'priceless'.

One drawback to using life insurance is the health require-ment to qualify. An old axiom used in the life insurance business is, "You buy life insurance with your health, and you pay for it with your money." All of the money in the world will not buy a policy if you are not healthy enough to satisfy the underwriting requirements. Another drawback is age. Life insurance premiums increase with age. Each birthday will add dollars to the cost of a policy. In most cases, a permanent plan of insurance is appropriate because of the permanent nature of the need and the level premium cost.

The amount of insurance you provide depends on your particular situation. A program can be designed to approx-imate the value of the agribusiness transitioned to active children. Rather than making all distributions equal, invest your effort in making your distributions just. Children are fortunate to receive any inheritance and you are generous to provide one. Becoming tied to exact formulas, and agonizing over dynamic numbers does not provide peace of mind or reward anyone involved. You can attempt to replicate the business value, then provide life insurance proceeds of equal value to your heirs, but how do you settle on that value?

Case Study

Ben Wallace owns a very successful irrigation design and installation business. Ben's daughter, Christy, will become the owner/manager over the next 10 years. Ben and Christy have designed a development plan that includes some college extension courses in hydro-engineering, crops, and personnel management. Christy Wallace will assume the estimating duties of the business with the oversight (mentoring relationship) of Skip Parker, the company's head engineer. Today the business is worth $2.1 million. Ben Wallace estimates that, over the next 10 years, the business will increase in value to about $5 million. With an increasing demand curve, continued water shortages, and increased power costs, the business could be worth $12 million in 20 years. Ben knows that these numbers are projections and that many factors play into the continued growth and development of the business.

Ben's son Justin is a junior executive for an accounting firm. He loves his work and enjoys raising his family in the city. As Ben implements his succession plan, he takes into account several factors. Given a business valuation of $2.1 million today and factoring in a nominal increase in business value due to normal business efforts, given Christy's apprenticeship during which she receives less than the going wage, and ignoring all other assets in the household, Ben plans to draft a buy/sell agreement between Christy and Justin Wallace. Christy Wallace is the beneficiary of a policy on the life of Ben. All household assets, including all business ownership interests, are to be split evenly in case Ben Wallace dies prematurely. Justin will be obligated to sell Christy his interest in the business as a result of any estate settlement. Christy will be required to buy all of Justin's business interests received as a result of Ben Wallace's untimely death. The buy/sell agreement sets a predetermined formula for the calculation of business value. It sets a sell/purchase price based on number of years in the future, net income, and the value of gross business assets.

There is no right, or perfect solution. In this case, Christy will have full ownership and control of the business. She will be compensated for her investment in the business. Justin will get his share of Ben's legacy in dollars, rather than business assets, which fits his lifestyle and career choice. Most of all, Ben is rewarded with a special form of parental satisfaction. He is helping each child realize a dream. He passes a legacy of opportunity, wealth, and care to subsequent generations.

SELLING TO ACTIVE CHILDREN

Some farm owners consider selling their business interest to their active children since the bulk of their wealth is tied up in assets of the business. Taking equity out of the business may be an imperative to support a retirement life style. An installment sale is relatively simple. It promotes equitable divisions of wealth, and it offers some positive tax benefits. When dealing with your sons, daughters, or extended family you can offer flexible terms. Installment sales allow you to control circumstances based on your needs and the buyer's limitations. A word of caution: the government scrutinizes any sale that appears to be a bargain. A sale allows you to fund the next venture in your vocational life, retirement, or provide for spousal support. At your death, the payments due, if not self-canceling, will pass to your heirs.

Case Study

Stephen DeCou owns 627 acres of almonds and walnuts, including a huller. His equipment allows him to tend not only to his own operation but also to those of several small farmers. Stephen's sons, Jeff, Carl, and David, all work in the business. Though they are close in age, the brothers have well-defined roles. They respect the abilities and limitations of each other and have created excellent supportive working relationships. Steve is ready to retire. "At 67, I've earned the right to do exactly what I want to do. It's time to cast off," he explains. That is exactly what he has been planning for 20 years. His next venture involves a converted 42-foot fishing troller in which he plans to cruise the inland waterways.

The DeCou boys are ready to assume full control of the business. Stephen wants to pass the business as a viable entity, but he does not want to give it away. As his only heirs, his sons will receive everything in time. Steve believes in giving the boys a fair opportunity, not a gift. "If they earn it, they'll appreciate it," he states. "Besides, I've got to look out for Nancy (his spouse) and me. After all, my Dad's still alive at 91!"

The entire operation, including land, business assets, equipment, and business operations (customer lists, commodity contracts, good name) is valued at $6.5 million. Stephen asks the boys to make a down payment of $1 million and pay the balance in installments. He offers them various opportunities, each with various tax benefits, payback provisions, and other considerations. The two methods that warrant a review, given this situation, are a self-canceling installment note (SCIN) or a private annuity (see Chapter 9.).

DESIGNING SUBSIDIARY OPPORTUNITIES

Most agribusiness operations are actually comprised of several potentially separate businesses. Consider an agribusiness that raises replacement heifers; puts-up hay for feed; grows row crops, pumpkins, gourds, and Indian corn for fall/Halloween decorations; offers custom harvesting; and operates a roadside produce stand. Each subsidiary may be operated as a separate entity from the whole. Operating separate subsidiaries offers several advantages. First, the subsidiary becomes a stand-alone profit center. Management is allowed a narrow-minded view of a single segment of the business. Growth and development plans are designed to focus strictly on a single operation. Unprofitable operations can be eliminated. Finally, with a family of active participants, splitting a large operation into subsidiaries allows the transition of each piece into separate ownership. Splitting off or separating subsidiary operations is important because your active children may have distinctly different philosophies or management strategies.

chapter 7
TRANSITION TO A LOYAL EMPLOYEE OR AN OUTSIDE PARTY

If no one in your immediate family is interested or capable of assuming an active role in your business operation, leaving your business to a loyal employee or an outside party may be the best option. A loyal employee may be your first choice, or you may consider an outside competitor or another business that wants to expand. There are many examples of family businesses that have outgrown the capabilities of family management. Stop and think about the full ramifications of the situation. A company is so successful that outside management or a corporate structure is needed.

NON-FAMILY MANAGEMENT SUCCESSOR

When no family member is interested in a management role either because your children established careers elsewhere and the grandchildren are still young, look at the current roster of loyal employees for management candidates. Use the candidate evaluation form found in the planning tools section (Chapter 5 – Leadership Skills Inventory). Does the candidate have what it takes to help the farm prosper? Groom the employee of your choice for a management position, and assume the role of mentor. You will eventually become a one-man board of directors, guiding the operation and initiating direction at arm's length.

If there is no loyal employee who could take over management, then start recruiting candidates, but first establish a specific position with a detailed job description and implied opportunities.

Management outside the family circle offers opportunities you may not realize with family members. An outside management candidate will not have the entitlement mindset of a family member. An outside candidate is often eager to learn, while family members may be complacent with the status quo. A non-family manager knows that employment is based on performance, attitude, and aptitude. A family member may think of employment as a genetic right.

You must ensure that a non-family manager is not confused as to who is in charge. The nature of a family farm may result in many people giving directions and advice or making demands. These demands may conflict with your directions. Your job as owner and mentor is to control the employee's work environment. Nothing is more frustrating than mixed messages and conflicting assignments.

Compensation of a non-family manager must be comparable with the prevailing marketplace wage and benefits. Many family businesses offer wage and benefit packages far below generally accepted wages. Low wages are often justified with ownership shares, informal bonuses, or comments such as "it is just the way we run the business." In other words, there are certain inherent rights in a family company. When an outside manager is hired, informality must give way to professionalism. A quality management candidate expects, and is entitled to, a wage commensurate with the responsibilities of the position. As an employer, your interests are best served with a competitive benefits package. With a competitive compensation package, you can attract and retain the best candidates.

A key to integrating a non-family manager successfully is communication. The role of communication in business is a clear articulation of the where, why, and how of strategic direction. Open communication with current employees, family members, the current owner, and the new manager is important. Communication by means of the spoken word, actions, inactions, and attitude must clearly inform everyone. You must be alert to verbal and nonverbal clues of discontent and dissension caused by bringing in an "outsider."

Communicate early and often. People need to feel informed. You must recognize that hiring an outside manager often shakes up the current pecking order. Your goal of integrating a new manager is greatly enhanced with effective communication and well-defined roles. Current employees and family members want to know what role they will fill when you bring in the new manager. Your job, again, is to formalize the business by defining roles and creating an environment that is dynamic yet structured for success.

Table 7-1. Action Plan—Hire an Excellent Manager Candidate

Topic	Description	Who	Date
Written job description.	Delineate a specific job description for the position for which you are hiring.	Owner/ manager	10/01-12/31
Skills/abilities.	Define the skills/abilities necessary to perform the duties of the job.	Owner/ manager	10/01-12/31
Active recruiting	When looking for the right person to fill the position, ask other farm owners, business leaders, competitors, and complementing businesses.	Owner/ manager	01/02-03/31
Employment agency.	Contact specialized employment agencies and enlist their assistance in your search.	Owner/ manager	01/02-03/31
Advertise.	Place advertisements in magazines, newspapers periodicals, association mailings, newsletters, and college alumni magazines.	Owner/ manager	01/02-03/31
Pre-screen applicants.	Compare résumés which outline experience, education, skills, and abilities. Compare these against the job description and requirements.	Owner/ manager	04/01-04/15
Contact references.	Contact and screen at least three references for each candidate.	Owner/ manager	04/01-04/15

Schedule and perform interviews.	Schedule and perform interviews to screen applicants. Rate each from 1-10. Determine which candidates will return for a second interview.	Owner/ manager	04/16-05/01
Perform second interviews. and pre-employment screening.	Perform second interviews and pre-employment screening. Schedule pre-employment tests such as drug screens.	Owner/ manager	05/02-05/15
Hire	Hire the candidate of your choice, schedule start date, define a development plan, and communicate with current employees and family members.	Owner/ manager	05/16-06/01

Note: For simplification we used "owner/manager" as the person responsible for every action. In reality, you may enlist the help of staff, other employees, and employment agencies, or appoint a hiring committee.

NEEDLE IN THE HAYSTACK

Finding talent is the biggest challenge of every business today. Finding the right person is like finding a needle in the haystack. I suggest you start with a detailed plan of action.

To get started on this process, first thoroughly detail a job description and then define the characteristics, skills, and abilities a person must have to fill the duties of the job description. I call this the "wanted poster." The characteristics become a picture of the person for whom you are looking. Measure the talents of each candidate against the needs elaborated in the job description. If you know what you want, you will find the person. Metaphorically hold up the wanted poster next to each candidate's résumé, and look for a match.

The best method for finding the right management candidate is active recruiting. Active recruiting means asking other farm owners, business leaders, competitors, and complementing businesses about qualified candidates. Recruiting includes the assistance of specialized employment search firms or ads in publications. When you are looking for the right fit, you do not want to overlook any opportunity. From a pool of quality prospects, you start the selection process—separating the wheat from the chaff.

WAGES AND BENEFITS

As long as the composition of employees is 100% family, wages and benefits are usually not a major topic for discussion. Dad or Mom dictate pay levels. Pay and benefits become more formal when you hire help from outside the family. Outside employees do not consider future ownership of the business a basis for lower pay. In hiring a management successor, all administrative factors of the business become more formal, especially those related to pay and benefits.

An employee handbook can guide discussions between you and your management candidate. This handbook is used to establish the parameters of a working relationship, including:

1. Job Description
2. Compensation
3. Benefits
4. Vacation and Sick Leave Guidelines
5. Performance Expectations
6. Code of Conduct
7. Review Processes
8. Bonus Systems

BOARD OF DIRECTORS OR FAMILY COUNCIL

In large business operations and corporations, a board of directors provides oversight, guidance, a think tank, a sounding board, and strategic direction. A board of directors is not as concerned with day-to-day business management, but instead with business direction and profitable growth. A board ratifies management decisions, suggests strategies, and promotes a global viewpoint. The board is a guide that gives ballast through the winds of change. A family business considering expansion, diversifying a product offering, adding formalized management, or hiring outside help should form a board of directors. It can be formally established under the articles of incorporation or less formally as a family council.

State laws and the articles of incorporation govern a board of directors. Rules are established to control the number of directors, the number of votes required to make certain decisions, meeting limitations, and business latitude. The shareholders (owners) of the corporation elect a board of directors. In a small family corporation, you may expect 100% of the ownership to be retained within the family. Large corporations have a diverse group of owners referred to as stockholders. An active board of directors in a corporate setting acts in the following capacity:

1. Elects/removes officers
2. Acts as a "sounding board"
3. Provides intellectual capital
4. Monitors financial status
5. Monitors business goals
6. Monitors personnel
7. Buffers unpopular decisions
8. Declares dividends
9. Reflects/discusses decisions
10. Provides objective advice
11. Expands networks/contacts
12. Monitors business performance
13. Monitors wages, benefits, and bonuses
14. Sets strategic direction

In many family agribusinesses the stockholders, management, and board of directors are often one and the same. If business growth and development are not important, this arrangement may allow a business to survive. If, on the other hand, expansion is important, then a true board of directors comprised of successful business people, educators, legal professionals, accounting specialists, retired business leaders, or representatives from a complimentary industry are critical for success. Like hiring an outside manager, creating a board of directors formalizes the business structure. It gives direction and causes a business to respond effectively to opportunities and challenges.

Large or small, creating a board of directors, or a family council, adds new dimensions to a business seeking opportunities to thrive in the fast-paced business climate now and in the future. One trade-off in adding a board of directors is relinquishing some control. You surrender sole control to gain a diverse point of view. The focus evolves from business as an extension of family to business as a vocation in which family participates. Family business is an emotional effort. Emotion is positive as a tie that binds, but it can also impede progress. A board of directors helps to make the business less emotional and more objective.

Family councils are designed to act as quasi–boards of directors. If you choose a family council, it should be designed with duties and responsibilities very similar to a board of directors. For a family council to be effective, the duties, rights, privileges, expectations, authority, and responsibilities should be in writing. The value of a family council is the synergy created by a diverse group of people focusing their talents and unique perspectives on the challenges of growing a business.

MANAGEMENT SUCCESSION

A board of directors, or a family council, becomes an integral participant in the management succession process through the following rules:

1. The board of directors/family council may first assist with a comprehensive job description. The board can screen resumes and narrow the pool of candidates to be interviewed.

2. A board of directors/family council can assist with development plans once a candidate is hired. It can facilitate an effective development plan, progressively granting responsibility and

authority as experience dictates.

3. A board of directors/family council can help smooth the management transition with introductions to important customers, third-party vendors, and loyal employees.

4. A board of directors/family council allows more exposure when you seek a management successor. Recall that recruiting is the best way to find a replacement, and the addition of several more eyes and ears multiplies your opportunities.

5. A board of directors/family council can smooth the management transition process. It can buffer you from undue pressure as a result of some of the decisions you make in the selection/transition process. Management is not a popularity contest, and your job will not always endear you to others.

6. Using a board of directors/family council can deflect the "fallout" from disgruntled participants. Everyone has an opinion and is entitled to share it, but you are not obligated to bow to the demands or bend to the wishes of others. The second opinion of a board of directors/family council allows you to make decisions that are best for all concerned—the business, the family, and you.

7. An active board of directors/family council can help to design a development plan. It then can act as a mentor to management candidates as they follow the steps delineated in the plan.

A member of the board of directors/family council has the advantage of working with your candidate from an arm's length.

8. A board of directors/family council member can be mentally removed from the crises of the moment and focus on the activities that will ensure a successful management successor.

ESTABLISHING A BOARD OF DIRECTORS OR A FAMILY COUNCIL

When exploring the option of establishing a board of directors, you must overcome the normal reluctance that accompanies any new idea. Most successful business leaders sincerely want to help other companies succeed. They pride themselves on meeting the challenges inherent in business today. Most business leaders would be honored to serve on your board of directors.

A big fear in establishing a board of directors may be sharing company business, which in a family owned business may mean family concerns. You risk being out-voted on important business issues. The initial temptation when establishing a board of directors is to invite people already close to your agribusiness, such as your accountant, attorney, or a third-party vendor. Though excellent choices, each may be inclined to share your opinions to maintain a business relationship. Appointing people who are too familiar or dependent on your business will not create the kind of diverse thought a varied group of individuals can.

Family should have a limited representation on the board. First, you represent the family's interest. Secondly, adding family weighs the board too much toward family issues. Finally, family members do not promote a diverse point of view.

The following recommendations may be helpful as you establish a board of directors/family council:

1. Define parameters for the board of directors. On what issues will the board be consulted? Describe the terms of commitment, the responsibility, and authority of the board of directors.

2. Screen and interview applicants as you would an important employee. Approach several successful board candidates; share your concepts, expectations, and the needs of your business. Solicit dialogue to decide if each candidate is the right fit for your business needs.

3. Communicate with all concerned, both active and passive family members. Employees should be informed of company management changes. A board of directors will formalize many company management functions.

A board of directors should be comprised of an odd number of people. It should have a sufficient number to assure diverse input on business decisions. Directors should commit to serve for a specific term such as two or three years. Terms should be staggered so that as you bring on new members, you maintain a historical point of reference.

LOYAL EMPLOYEES MAKE A DIFFERENCE

Maintaining support of loyal employees in any business transition is critical. Loyal employees may provide the backbone of consistency in your business. They may constitute profitable systems of operation; most importantly, they may be a well of intellectual capital, historical perspective, and living vision that could take years to replace. Questions to consider are listed below.

- Is planning for succession important?
- Is your business plan designed to implement a succession plan?
- Is your family prepared, informed, and supportive?
- Will you consider related as well as unrelated successors?
- Is company ownership titled for succession?
- Have you designed a plan for candidate development?
- Have you considered a board of directors or a family council?
- Have you arranged for equitable transfers to passive heirs?
- Do you have a contingency plan spousal support? Have you thoroughly communicated your succession intentions and developed a communication process for each phase of implementation?

part3
ESTATE PLANNING IN A COMPREHENSIVE SUCCESSION PLAN

No one lives forever! Financial devastation is the latent crisis that awaits a farmer's spouse and immediate heirs by not planning for the sudden catastrophe of death or disability. The laws of intestate succession—dying without a will—prevent efficient handling of estate taxes and inheritance obligations. Intestate succession never represent a person's wants, hopes, or dreams.

chapter 8
ESTATE PLANNING

Estate planning is an integral part of a comprehensive succession plan. The function of estate planning is to transfer your assets, including your business interests, efficiently while minimizing your estate tax obligation. An estate plan is designed to minimize transfer obligations while maximizing retained capital. Estate planning insures the outcome of your plans despite the length of your life or any disastrous contingency that may imperil your long-term goals.

Proper estate planning is a crucial part of a well-designed succession plan. A comprehensive succession plan is implemented during life. A complete plan transfers your farm to a successor. If you are among those farm owners who maintain a fractional ownership interest in the farm, estate planning appropriately transfers that interest and ensures financial support for a spouse (or other special needs) at your death.

A succession plan focuses on a systematic transfer of ownership to successive generations as you anticipate retirement or the next venture in your vocational life. The focal point of ownership succession is a predetermined transfer to your daughters, sons, co-owners, loyal employees, or other third parties.

Estates are nothing more than an accumulation of property. A person's estate is the collection of all assets owned at the moment of death. Since you cannot take it with you, the property you own at death must be distributed. Estate planning is the design of that distribution.

Special care is taken in drafting your estate plan to make sure that it complements and does not conflict with your ownership succession plan. Many of the issues addressed in the ownership succession plan overlap with those in the estate plan.

PROPERTY TRANSFERS

Property is divided into two asset classes, real and personal. Personal property is further divided into tangible and intangible. Real property is real estate. The farm, land, buildings, permanent crops, or anything that is permanently attached to the land is real estate. Personal property that you can touch is tangible. Intangible personal property represents something of value. An example of intangible personal property is a stock certificate in a corporation. The certificate itself has little, if any, value but could potentially represent multiple shares of one of America's finest businesses.

Property may be sold or exchanged, given away, or distributed as a bequest at death. A person has the right to sell or exchange property at any time for something of value or consideration. In estate planning, the sale of property does not necessarily remove the asset from the estate; it merely replaces one asset for another. The property transferred may be removed, but the money received replaces the asset. Property given away to another person removes the asset from the estate. Gifted property must follow certain guidelines to qualify as completed gifts. Property not otherwise sold or gifted, that is, property that is owned by a person at death, is a part of a person's estate. Property in an estate is distributed at death according to a will, right of survivorship, contract, trust, beneficiary designation, or laws of intestacy in the state of residence.

IT COSTS MONEY TO DIE

Final expenses, including medical charges; funeral expenses; outstanding bills; estate taxes; and fees for probate, an attorney, the court, and the appraisal, can be prohibitively expensive. Estate taxes and transfer obligations are an onerous burden for any substantial estate.

An estate tax worksheet may look similar to the following:

Gross estate	$_____
Funeral and administration expensed	$_____
Debt and outstanding taxes	$_____
Losses	$_____
Total deductions	$
Adjusted gross estate	$_____
Marital deduction	$_____
Charitable deduction	$_____
Total deductions	$_____
Taxable estate	$_____
Adjusted taxable gifts	$_____
Tentative tax base	$_____
Tentative tax	$_____

Gift taxes payable $_____
Estate tax payable before credits $_____
Tax credits $_____
Applicable credit amount $_____
State death tax credit $_____
Foreign death tax credit $_____
Gift tax credit pre-1977 $_____
Credit on prior transfers $_____
   Total credit $_____
   Net federal estate tax payable $_____

An estate plan is designed to minimize your estate tax burden while maximizing the amount of assets you transfer to your beneficiaries. Though there are laws that help farmers and other family business owners with favorable tax payment arrangements, estate taxes are still an onerous burden to the beneficiary.

Combining probate fees, an estimate for last medical expenses, funeral costs, and outstanding debt, it is not uncommon to see a cash administrative cost of as much as 5% of the gross estate. Final expenses can add up to a significant cash outlay from the proceeds of an estate. The following table is not an unrealistic estimate of estate taxes and transfer obligations.

Table 8-1. Estimated Estate Settlement Costs

Gross Estate	Estimated Administrative Expenses	Estimated Estate Tax	Total Estate Tax/Transfer Obligations
$2,000,000	$100,000	$390,000	$490,000
$5,000,000	$250,000	$1,782,500	$2,032,500
$10,000,000	$500,000	$4,110,000	$4,610,000
$15,000,000	$750,000	$6,437,500	$7,187,500
$20,000,000	$1,000,000	$6,437,500	$9,765,000

In financial planning it is said:
"Most people do not plan to fail, they fail to plan."

So if it costs money to die, what options are available to pay the estate tax and transfer obligations? How can a person satisfy financial obligations, provide security for the family, and maximize the legacy left to the next generation?

OPTION 1: SELL THE FARM

One option is to sell the farm to satisfy the estate settlement costs. A simple buy/sell agreement may serve as the mechanism to transition the farm to a new owner. A buy/sell agreement is a formalized agreement between a farmer, seller, and the successive buyer, in which the farmer agrees to sell and the successive owner agrees to buy. The buy/sell agreement is a simple succession plan used in conjunction with the estate plan.

A buy/sell agreement can provide cash for estate settlement costs and the support necessary for a spouse and dependents. It allows the farm to transition to the ownership successor of your choice. A buy/sell agreement is a contractual obligation in which you agree to sell and your successor agrees to buy. The typical buy/sell agreement is predicated on death to trigger the buy/sell transaction, but some may include a provision for disability. The agreement specifies the method of valuation used to establish the buy/sell price. The agreement addresses any specific conditions pertinent to the sale, such as monthly payments for income needs or a lump sum payment to allow your dependents more financial flexibility. A family needs time and money to adjust to the dual catastrophes of the loss of a loved one and a dramatic change in lifestyle.

Key Point: Business Value

Fair market value is the price for which a business interest would sell between a willing buyer and a willing seller. It is assumed that both buyer and seller have full knowledge of all of the pertinent facts of the business with equal negotiating ability, neither one being under any obligation to buy or sell.

A closely held business interest, a corporation not listed on a stock exchange, such as a partial interest in a family corporation, is not easy to value. If there is a ready-market for a partial interest in a closely held business, the value is easily ascertained. Since there is no ready-market, a partial ownership interest is not easily valued, so the appraised value is significantly less than a full ownership interest.

Partial ownership interests can be discounted further based on a majority or minority interest. A minority interest is worth less than a majority interest. Since a minority interest has little, if any, control over management decisions, a willing seller may have to discount severely the price to a buyer.

A buy/sell agreement is usually funded with life insurance. A life insurance policy covering the life of the farmer, with the successor owner as beneficiary, ensures that money is available when needed. A predetermined amount of life insurance is usually an educated guess based on a future business value. Some flexibility must be allowed since most buy/sell agreements specify a current appraisal.

A buy/sell agreement allows your farm to pass outside the provisions of your will, though the asset value of the farm, or the money received, is included in your estate. Without a buy/sell agreement, the farm is distributed according to the provisions of your will.

OPTION 2: SELL THE FARM AT DEATH

What if you just do not want to sell the farm? Not only do you not want to sell the farm, you do not want to discuss any plan that involves an ownership transition. Consider the consequences of failing to make a decision.

A decision to do nothing:
- *Feels* like procrastination
- *Sounds* like stubbornness
- *Acts* like an attempt to stall the inevitable

The unavoidable fallout caused by failing to form a plan causes an overwhelming burden... just when your family is least able to cope. Mom wants to see the farm pass to your son, but he may still be too young to assume responsibility. You have made no provision for interim management, successor development, or the financial welfare of your spouse and dependents. You may effectively leave your farm with insufficient capitalization, which fails to support the financial needs of the business.

OPTION 3: PASS THE FARM THROUGH A WILL

A bequest is using the provisions of a will to transition your farm to the next generation. Three issues must be addressed with a transfer as a bequest.

- How will you provide financial support for your spouse and dependents? Is there a provision for their continued support?
- Is there a provision to satisfy the onerous estate taxes and transfer obligations associated with a bequest? Though a bequest is an alternative, the implication is not that you do nothing. That is irresponsible. As a smart businessperson, a caring family patriarch/matriarch, and a United States citizen, your responsibility is to minimize the estate tax and transfer obligations imposed on the settlement of your estate.
- Is there a business plan? You should prepare the business operation by implementing a sound business plan—a plan that will allow for a solid opportunity as the new owner succeeds you.

If ownership succession is left as a provision in a will, significant conflicts can surface. To maintain financial survival, your spouse will be forced to make the difficult decisions you would not. Most spouses find themselves precariously poised between the aspirations of the children and the need to survive economically. Your children need money, flexibility, and the option of accepting risk. Your spouse needs stability, security, and an assured level of financial support. She may not be willing to subject herself to any more risk than is absolutely necessary.

An ownership transition triggered by a will is often the trigger for family conflict. Sibling rivalries can be strong, even in grown children. Now add a business with shared ownership between active and passive children– each faction with its own opposing objectives. Active, working family members want as much earned capital as possible reinvested into the business to promote business growth.

To active children, who are already assured of a paycheck sufficient for family obligations, the financial strength of the business is a much higher priority.

Passive family members, those working outside the family business, want income. They want a return on this significant asset—their interest in the agribusiness. Carrying this asset on their balance sheet only serves as a reminder that investments should return interest, dividends, or equity. In this case, equity growth of the business exacerbates the problem because as the asset appreciates, there is still no way to receive equity in cash. It reinforces the fact that they are owners of a valuable asset that can never be converted to money.

LIFE INSURANCE

Equitable transfers to siblings can be provided with life insurance. It can provide money to support the family and satisfy other financial obligations. Estate taxes and transfer obligations can be paid with life insurance benefits. It can also support the capital needs of the business. One of the reasons most businesses fail when passed from one generation to the next is insufficient capital. A well-designed life insurance plan may solve this problem.

Selling the farm may be your choice; keep in mind, timing is everything. Selling out of desperation or during a down market makes a bad situation worse. Life insurance can provide working capital to keep the business afloat while decisions are made or the market improves.

ECONOMIC GROWTH AND TAX RELIEF RECONCILIATION ACT OF 2001 (EGTRRA)

Planning around changing tax laws is like trying to hit a moving target. With the changing dynamics of family, the cyclical nature of business, and the proliferation of new laws, you must refine your estate plan on an annual basis. There is no such thing as "once and done" in estate planning.

The EGTRRA of 2001 is designed to increase the applicable exclusion amount incrementally—the amount a person can exclude from estate tax through a transfer to others. It gradually reduces the estate tax imposed on a person's estate, allowing a greater value to pass to your heirs. By 2009, the applicable exclusion amount will top out at $3.5 million, allowing a person to pass up to that amount to their heirs free of estate tax. In 2010, the estate tax is slated for repeal so no estate tax may be due during that year. On January 1, 2011, the provisions of EGTRRA are slated to "sunset." The applicable exclusion amount will revert back to the pre-EGTRRA amount of $1 million. The other provisions of the law—a gradual reduction in the gift tax to a low of 35% and an incremental increase in the generation-skipping transfer tax exemption to mirror the applicable exclusion amount—will sunset on December 31, 2010.

The following table demonstrates the estimated estate tax or capital gains tax your heir may be obligated to pay as a result of the provisions of EGRTTA. My example highlights a $7,320,500 estate and a 10% annual growth rate. I assume a 20% capital gains tax rate, tax rates per the current EGTRRA schedule ($1,000,000 cost basis).

Table 8-2. Estimated Estate Taxes or Capital Gains Taxes by Year

Year	Estate Size	Exemption	Estate Tax Due	
2005	7,320,500	1,500,000	2,725,635	
2006	8,052,550	2,000,000	2,784,173	
2007	8,857,805	2,000,000	3,086,012	
2008	9,743,586	2,000,000	3,484,613	
2009	10,717,944	3,500,000	3,248,075	
2010	11,789,738	Estate tax repealed	**Capital Gains Tax** $1,897,948	
2011	12,968,712	1,000,000	**Current Law** 6,576,227	**Capital Gains** 2,133,742
2012	14,265,584	1,000,000	7,354,350	2,393,117
2013	15,692,142	1,000,000	8,210,285	2,678,428
2014	17,261,356	1,000,000	9,147,946	2,992,271
2015	18,987,492	1,000,000	10,097,320	3,337,498

As you can see, EGTRRA does not eliminate the estate tax. It may decrease the cost to settle your estate over the next few years. Still, the law does not eliminate settlement costs and transfer obligations. The capital gains tax imposed in 2010, though only about one-half of the estate tax, is a significant cash outlay for the settlement of most estates.

CONGRESS AND EGTRRA

The current laws governing estate taxes, gift taxes, and generation-skipping transfer taxes are scheduled to sunset on December 31, 2010. If Congress fails to act, pre-EGTRRA tax levels will be reinstated on January 1, 2011. It is not wise for you to expect the actions of our legislature to uphold the integrity of your estate plan. I recommend that you assume Congress will not act, the law will sunset, and estate limits and tax rates will return to their pre-EGTRRA levels. Planning is about anticipating, be it for an estate, a business, owner succession, or retirement; it must involve contingencies. It is wise to plan for the worst, but hope for the best.

WILLS, PROBATE, AND ESTATE SETTLEMENT

Estate planning using trusts, beneficiary designations, contracts, and lifetime gifts make it possible to minimize probate. An estate settled with a will through probate is subject to public scrutiny. Any estate settlement made using your will is subject to probate. The process is lengthy. It can take six months to settle a simple estate—sometimes longer. There are several ways to avoid probate:

1. *Contract terms.* The terms of a contract may specify transfer provisions.
2. *Operation of Law.* Property passes from one owner to the next based on the terms of the title. The right of survivorship entitles the survivor to receive the property regardless of what may be stated in the will of the decedent.
3. *Beneficiary designations.* Proceeds from life insurance, retirement accounts, and other financial instruments may be distributed according to beneficiary designation. Beneficiary designations supersede the stipulations of a will.
4. *Lifetime gifts.* Lifetime gifts pass outside of the probate process. (Do not confuse the probate process with the calculation of estate tax

obligations. Gifts may be brought back into the estate for the calculation for estate taxes.)

5. *Living trusts.* Assets titled in the name of a trust are not subject to probate.
6. *Transfer on death.* Transfer on death is a provision authorized in some states that permit securities to pass automatically to a named beneficiary.

The basic purpose of a will is to avoid intestate succession (dying without directions for the distribution of your property). Probate is the process of settling an estate.

A will allows you to:
1. Designate a legal guardian for minor children.
2. Name the executor of your estate.
3. Make bequests to individuals.
4. Create a trust for the disposition of certain assets. (Trusts are used to benefit minor children, consider special needs, and provide a way to reduce estate taxes and transfer obligations.)

The trust created by your will, a testamentary trust, is no different than a living, or *inter vivos*, trust created during your lifetime. The form and function are basically the same. Finally, a will allows for peace of mind because you completed something that positively affects multiple generations. The estate planning you do today results in the legacy you leave tomorrow.

TRUSTS

Trusts may be summarized as follows:
1. Trusts are integral to estate planning.

2. Trusts are devices that own and manage assets.
3. The premise of a trust is the transfer of property. by a grantor to the trust where it is held, managed, and distributed according to the directions established in the trust document.
4. A trust is established for the benefit of a trust beneficiary.
5. The trustee as fiduciary manages the trust assets. The trustee, or fiduciary, may be a person or an institution such as a bank or trust company.
6. A person can transfer all or any portion of their estate to a trust.
7. A trust established during the grantor's life is an inter vivos trust. A trust made at death or through the provisions of a will is a testamentary trust.
8. A trust can also be irrevocable (cannot be changed, altered, or amended) or revocable (subject to the discretion of the grantor).
9. The nature of a trust is very discretionary, depending on the situation a person is trying to address.
10. Trusts are used as often for a management tool; they relieve a grantor of management power, as they are for estate tax benefits.

REVOCABLE TRUSTS

A revocable trust allows the grantor the opportunity to change his or her mind. The grantor of a revocable trust has the right to change, amend, cancel, or otherwise affect the conditions of the trust. Due to the revocable nature of the trust, the transfer of property is not a "completed transfer." Since the grantor retains control over the assets of the trust, the transfer is not complete so many of the estate tax benefits often associated with trust are lost. A revocable trust does offer some distinct advantages:

1. Assets are managed.
2. A grantor, with the ability to act if necessary, can monitor the performance of the trustee.
3. Local ownership for out-of-state properties is provided.
4. A sole proprietorship or partnership interest can perpetuate the business in case of the death of the grantor.
5. It becomes irrevocable upon the death of the grantor, and property passes to the beneficiary outside of probate.

IRREVOCABLE TRUSTS

Irrevocable means that the trust cannot be changed, amended, altered, or canceled. Once a property is transferred to an irrevocable trust, it is a completed gift, and the transaction reduces the size of the grantor's estate. The reduction of estate causes a subsequent reduction in the estate tax, capital gains tax, and the probate fees. The biggest disadvantage to an irrevocable trust is relinquishing control of an asset. Most people are very hesitant to give up control of a valuable asset that may have taken years to acquire. The advantages to using an irrevocable trust include:

1. It reduces the size of the estate with a corresponding reduction in the estate tax obligation.

2. Assets can be managed, especially those requiring a special level of or vocational expertise.
3. Assets pass to the beneficiary outside the probate process.
4. The grantor's creditors cannot claim trust property.
5. Beneficiaries must negotiate with the trustee regarding matters of the trust since the grantor has no control. This advantage frees the grantor of undue pressure to alter or change the trust provisions.
6. It can protect the assets intended for the benefit of the children of a prior marriage from the discretion of a current spouse.

Table 8-3. Comparison of Simple and Complex Trusts

Simple Trusts	Complex Trusts
Must distribute income to all beneficiaries	Requires or allows the trustee to accumulate money
May limit distributions other than current income.	Allows the distribution of principal
Cannot make charitable donations	Allows for charitable donations

MARITAL DEDUCTION

Estate planning is about efficiently dividing assets according your wishes. Minimizing estate tax obligations and maximizing the assets you pass to your heirs are the primary functions of estate planning. The marital deduction allows a person to pass all assets to a spouse without triggering an estate tax obligation. It allows for some estate planning latitude as a person attempts to meet the three broad estate planning objectives. There are basically three ways in which to use the marital deduction to reduce your estate tax obligation.

1. *Leave everything to a spouse ("A trust").* Leaving everything to a spouse is a very simple and inexpensive (at least at the first death) estate planning strategy. Your spouse retains full control over the disposition of all assets in the estate. Assets placed in an A trust allow a surviving spouse total control. Though convenient, this does not use the applicable exclusion amount, so it may prove to be a haphazard estate planning alternative. It increases estate taxes since one spouse controls all of the assets in a household, many of which may appreciate between the first and second death. The total estate tax obligation may increase. This alternative defers the estate tax obligation; it does not reduce or eliminate the tax.

2. *Leave property valued at an amount equal to the applicable exclusion amount to another entity with the balance to your spouse ("B trust").* If you use a B trust, or a credit shelter trust, you pass an amount equal to the annual exclusion amount into the trust at the time of the first death. All other assets of the estate over the applicable exclusion amount pass to your spouse. Commonly referred to as a bypass trust, a spouse can use the assets of the trust for health, education, maintenance, and support.

3. *A combination of an "A and B trust"* is another
    way of saying, establish an A trust (marital trust),
    a B trust (bypass trust), and a C trust (qualified
    terminable interest property trust or QTIP).

Current Assets

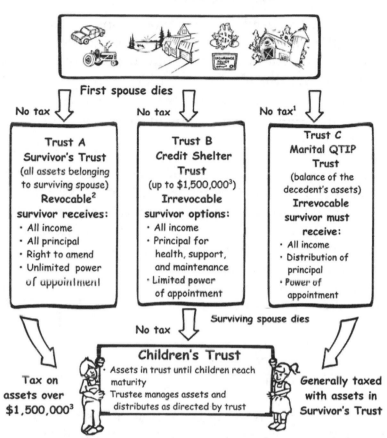

First spouse dies

No tax ⬇   No tax ⬇   No tax[1] ⬇

| Trust A Survivor's Trust (all assets belonging to surviving spouse) Revocable[2] survivor receives: • All income • All principal • Right to amend • Unlimited power of appointment | Trust B Credit Shelter Trust (up to $1,500,000[3]) Irrevocable survivor options: • All income • Principal for health, support, and maintenance • Limited power of appointment | Trust C Marital QTIP Trust (balance of the decedent's assets) Irrevocable survivor must receive: • All income • Distribution of principal • Power of appointment |

Surviving spouse dies

No tax ⬇

Children's Trust
• Assets in trust until children reach maturity
• Trustee manages assets and distributes as directed by trust

Tax on assets over $1,500,000[3]

Generally taxed with assets in Survivor's Trust

---

[1] The executor may choose to have the QTIP trust taxed at either death - first spouse or surviving spouse.

[2] Trust may be irrevocable for either a general power of appointment trust or an estate trust.

[3] The applicable exclusion amount ($1.5 million in 2005) is the dollar value of assets protected from federal estate tax by an individual's applicable credit amount. It is scheduled to change as follows: $2 million for 2006-2008; $3.5 million for 2009; zero federal estate tax for the year 2010; and $1 million for 2011 and thereafter (unless permanently repealed or otherwise modified).

"A TRUST"—MARITAL TRUST

Leaving all property to a spouse postpones estate taxes. Under the unlimited marital deduction, a person may pass all of his or her assets to a spouse without estate taxes. Though easy, this alternative underutilizes the estate tax laws. It does not allow a person to take advantage of the applicable exclusion amount. The law currently allows you to pass, or shelter, $1.5 million in assets to another person estate tax free. (Under EGTRRA in 2005, this amount increases incrementally through 2010.) Since your spouse automatically receives assets estate tax free, you miss the opportunity to remove the applicable exclusion amount from your gross estate. Even though your estate is not subject to estate tax on the first death, you may have missed the opportunity to shelter, estate tax- free, a portion of your assets. A couple may consider these alternatives under two circumstances:

- If the couple has little or no assets to pass
- If the surviving spouse needs all of the assets for financial support

The marital trust is designed to hold assets that exceed the applicable exclusion amount. Assets transferred to a marital trust avoid estate tax at the first death. The property is included in the estate of the second spouse. There are three common types of marital trusts:

1. *GENERAL POWER OF APPOINTMENT TRUST.* The general power of appointment trust allows the surviving spouse to transfer the property of the trust to anyone of his or her choosing. The general power of appointment trust must meet the following requirements:

- All trust accounting income is payable to the surviving spouse annually.
- The surviving spouse is granted a general power of appointment over the assets of the trust. The power of appointment allows the surviving spouse to determine who receives the assets at some time in the future.
- The trust is generally required to hold only assets that produce income. If the trust holds an unproductive asset, the trustee may be required to convert it to a productive asset.

2. *ESTATE TRUST.* The biggest advantage of the estate trust, over the general power of appointment trust, is that the estate trust can hold assets that do not necessarily generate income. The following criteria are required for an estate trust:
   - Assets of the trust, or income derived from the assets, may be distributed to the surviving spouse at the trustee's discretion.
   - At the second death, the remaining trust assets and any undistributed income must be included in the estate of the surviving spouse.

3. *QUALIFIED TERMINABLE INTEREST PROPERTY (QTIP) TRUST.* The basis of the QTIP trust is an income for your spouse during his or her lifetime, but you retain control over who receives a controlling interest in the property upon the death of your spouse. The biggest drawback, as we discuss the QTIP trust, is the requirement that the assets produce an income. If your farm is not an income-producing

asset, your surviving spouse could require the trustee to sell the property to convert it to an income-producing asset. So, on one hand, you are assured the property will go to your designated beneficiary. On the other hand, it may be converted into stock to meet the income requirement. A QTIP trust must meet the following criteria:

- All trust accounting income is payable to the surviving spouse annually.
- No one is allowed a power of appointment over the assets of the trust during the life of your surviving spouse. Only through a special power of appointment may the surviving spouse change the allocation of the assets placed in a QTIP upon his or her death. Otherwise the design of a QTIP is to insure that assets, specifically your farm, placed in this kind of trust pass to the beneficiary of your choosing. This happens despite the feelings or misgivings of a spouse after your death.
- The trust may hold unproductive, non-income generating assets for a reasonable period. This is to make it productive or convert it to a productive asset.
- The executor must elect on the estate tax return to have the property qualify for the marital deduction.

"B TRUST"—BYPASS OR CREDIT SHELTER TRUST

The second alternative is leaving an amount equal to the applicable exclusion amount to a person or entity other than a spouse then using the marital deduction to eliminate, or reduce, an estate tax obligation. For instance, you may leave an amount equal to the applicable exclusion amount, $1.5 million for 2005 to a bypass trust. The balance of your estate is left to your spouse. In this example, the amount left in the bypass trust ($1.5 million) is not subject to estate tax. The balance of your estate transfers to your spouse estate tax free.

The bypass trust is designed to hold assets up to the applicable exclusion amount to pass estate tax free. The assets must not also qualify for the marital deduction. The trust should be designed to allow your spouse access to the assets without disqualifying the trust.

The trust can be designed to allow your spouse beneficial use of the assets under certain conditions. A spouse may be entitled to a life income, certain powers of appointment (the power to give the assets to others), the right to receive money for his or her health, education, maintenance, and support and a non-cumulative right to withdraw up to $5,000 or 5% annually. Limiting a spouse's power to these rights satisfies the requirement that causes the trust property to avoid being considered under the marital deduction. The property in the bypass trust is not subject to estate tax at your death or upon the death of your spouse. Appreciating assets are suited for inclusion in the bypass trust. The future appreciation is removed from your estate.

"A-B TRUST"—A TWO-TRUST SHELTER

A popular estate planning device for a couple is the A-B trust, a two-trust structure. The structure of the A-B trust is simple. The applicable exclusion amount of $1.5 million is placed in a trust referred to as a bypass or credit shelter. (It shelters the applicable exclusion amount.) The balance of your estate is passed to your spouse, under the marital deduction, thereby passing the assets of your estate tax free. You may also place the assets passed under the marital deduction into a trust, commonly referred to as a marital trust.

> ### Case Study
>
> Ted and Samantha own a small berry farm. They hold some mutual funds for a rainy day. They own a cabin on the lake and other miscellaneous assets for a combined net estate of $3.5 million. If Ted dies in 2005, his will provides for the testamentary (after death) establishment of a bypass (credit shelter) trust in which $1.5 million (equal to the applicable exclusion amount) will be placed. The $2.0 million balance will pass to Samantha in a marital trust. Utilizing the A-B trust allows the entire estate of $3.5 million to pass to Ted's heir completely estate tax free.

The use of trusts in estate planning is as varied as there are estate planning attorneys and financial advisors. An informed consumer should feel comfortable with the basic concepts of the most commonly used trusts. You should understand the language of a trust discussion as it relates to your estate planning options.

IRREVOCABLE LIFE INSURANCE TRUST (ILIT)

Life insurance may be a component of your estate plan. It can provide the liquidity necessary to satisfy estate taxes and settlement obligations. An improperly written life insurance policy may cause the proceeds to be subject to inclusion in one's estate, compounding an already burdensome estate tax problem. An ILIT is designed to keep life insurance proceeds out of your estate. An ILIT is an "irrevocable" trust. The grantor maintains no power to alter, amend, or revoke the trust. Once established, you cannot change or alter beneficiaries or any other provisions of the trust. Any control you attempt to exercise, following establishment of the trust, may cause an incident of ownership. An incident of ownership signifies a grantor-controlled interest, which subjects the proceeds to inclusion in your estate. Most professional advisors recommend an ILIT to own life insurance in estate planning situations.

LIFE INSURANCE IN YOUR ESTATE PLAN

Deciding how much life insurance one should carry is dependent on a number of factors, including immediate cash needs, continuing spousal support, and special needs.

A key consideration in designing a life insurance program is keeping the death benefit out of your estate. The last thing a person intends to do is unwittingly increase their estate tax exposure by causing life insurance death benefit to be included in an estate at death. An ILIT, as a part of your estate plan, effectively removes the ownership of the life insurance policy from your estate. This allows the death benefit to pass to your beneficiaries' estate tax free. A partnership, or an LLC, may also own the life insurance on your life.

A basic life insurance analysis may help you to quantify your need for life insurance. Each person's situation is different, and every individual is unique. All businesses have varying degrees of financial need. Review the following list, and try to quantify your own life insurance needs. Life insurance provides money at the time when it is needed most for:

Life Insurance Financial Requirements

Final expenses, including funeral costs and medical expenses. $_____

Outstanding debts, including all outstanding debts, car loans, and mortgages. $_____

Specific needs, including provisions for a child with special needs, parents who may someday depend on our ability to help either with financial support or medical care, or other specific cash needs. $_____

Educational funds, including a fund established to provide educational support for your children, grand-children, or your spouse who may want to improve his or her education in order to re-enter the job market.
                                                   $_____

Income replacement so that your income, as sole bread winner, will be replaced in case of your untimely death. Income replacement can be based on a number of years such as, five years at $85,000, which equals $425,000, or you can provide a fund to replace your income for life such as; $85,000 income divided by an estimated investment rate of return of 7% equals $1,214,000.
                                                   $_____

Business overhead fund—a fund designed to compensate for the estimated extra expenses that may be incurred as a result of your absence. Estimate an amount of

---

money that may allow your survivors to hire extra help, special services, or a third-party consultant to assist with operations. This fund can pay for payroll, business expenses, or additional personnel. It may allow some breathing room as your heirs prepare the business for sale or transition. This fund can also be used to offset the sales price difference between a sale at fair market value and a "fire" sale. $_____

Estate tax and transfer obligations, including an estimate for estate tax and potential gift tax. $_____

Administrative expenses/probate fees, including fees to the executor and other professionals assisting in the settlement of your estate. A rule-of-thumb for executor's fees is 5%–10% of your gross estate. $_____

Equitable transfer fund—a fund established to pro-vide for equitable transfers to passive children. As part of your succession plan, you should consider transferring ownership of your agribusiness only to active children. As a gesture of care, love, and fairness, plan for an equitable transfer of assets to your passive children.
$_____

Total life insurance required $_____

Less current life insurance $_____

Life insurance shortfall $_____

chapter 9
IMPORTANT OPTIONS

Consider some of the following techniques to reduce your estate tax burden:

1. *Lifetime gifts.* Each person is entitled to make annual gifts of $11,000 to anyone. Currently, a married couple can combine gifts for a total of $22,000 to any number of people.
2. *Marital transfers.* Assets transferred to or gifted to a spouse are not subject to estate tax upon the death of the first spouse. Gifts or transfers to a spouse allow for a deferral of the estate tax until the surviving spouse dies.
3. *Charitable transfers.* Either at death or during life, charitable gifts can reduce the estate size, thus reducing the estate tax burden. Charitable gifts during life may also provide an income tax deduction.
4. *Credit shelter trusts.* A credit shelter trust is one of the most efficient ways to reduce estate taxes. Credit shelter trusts are established to own assets equal to the applicable exclusion amount ($1.5 million for 2005, $2.0 million for 2006-2008, $3.5 million for 2009, 0 for 2010, then $1.0 million for 2011 and beyond).
5. *Private annuity/self-canceling installment note.* Using an annuity or a self-canceling installment note to sell an asset (the farm) to a younger generation. The asset is sold, removing it from

the estate. The note (or annuity) is canceled upon death so the replacing asset (note/annuity) is effectively removed from the estate.

6. *Life insurance trust.* Using an irrevocable life insurance trust, an estate owner can reduce a current estate while creating a much larger asset outside of the estate. The premiums reduce the estate. The trust vehicle owns the life insurance outside of the estate to avoid subjecting the proceeds to estate taxes upon death.

GIFTING FOR THE AGRIBUSINESS OWNER

Gifting is the act of giving property to another person or entity. Most estate plans include a gifting program in which you gift property assets to your heirs on a systematic basis. The purpose of a gifting program is to reduce the size of your estate. Gifting reduces potential estate taxes while transferring ownership to your heirs without incurring a gift tax.

Gifting serves a three-fold purpose in your estate plan:
- First, it eliminates estate taxes on the amount of the gift.
- Second, it removes property from your estate.
- Finally, gifting appreciating property reduces your estate tax burden by eliminating the estate tax on future appreciation.

If you are married at the time of the gift, you can take advantage of gift-splitting. Gift-splitting essentially doubles your exclusion amount, which is the amount you are allowed to gift. Your applicable exclusion amount for gifting is $1.5 million or $3.0 million (for 2004 and 2005) if you use gift-splitting.

GIFTS TO REDUCE ESTATE TAX AND TRANSFER OBLIGATIONS

People are allowed to gift up to $11,000 annually to as many individuals as they want. You are encouraged to gift to any number of your heirs annually. This transfers your property and reduces your estate tax burden. Gift-splitting is also allowed in an annual gifting program. That means you and your spouse are allowed to remove $22,000 a year from your estate for each heir. An annual gifting program systematically reduces your estate tax and transfer obligations by removing the value of the gift from your estate. Further reductions are realized by removing assets that may experience significant appreciation.

Consistently appreciating property is like a caterpillar chewing on the leaves of your estate plan. The best plan may be chewed apart steadily as the caterpillar of appreciation continues to work methodically day and night, increasing the values of your assets. This appreciation increases your estate tax burden, which, in turn, increases the need to implement estate reduction techniques while reducing the effectiveness of your estate plan.

GIFTS OF FUTURE INTEREST

A gift can be rendered ineffective if the gift is of future interest. A future interest gift is simply a gift in which the heir is restricted from use, possession, benefit, or enjoyment of the property. If a gift is deemed of future interest, it remains in your estate. Your gift must be a complete transfer. The new owner, your heir, must be able to use, possess, benefit, and enjoy the gift freely. He or she must be free to transfer or sell the gift without restriction.

GIFTS IN TRUST

The transfer of property in trust encompasses two important points: the income interest created by the trust and the remainder interest of the trust. The income interest from a trust may qualify for the annual gift exclusion, if the income is distributed automatically to the beneficiary without condition. The remainder interest in a trust may not qualify as a completed gift if the creator of the trust, the trustor, maintains control of the trust assets.

A gift in trust will treat each beneficiary to the trust as a separate person. The terms of the trust dictate whether the trust counts for a present interest trust or a future interest trust. If a trustee is required to distribute all of the income from a trust annually, then the trust income qualifies as a gift. If, on the other hand, the trustor retains discretionary power over the trust, the trust does not qualify as a complete gift. Therefore, it is ineligible for the gift tax exclusion. Likewise, if the provisions of the trust dictate payouts based on certain events, the trust is not a completed gift. You should not use a trust to exercise control over an asset you intend to gift. You must unconditionally surrender all control and beneficial use of any property intended to qualify for the annual gift tax exclusion.

> ### Case Study
> Wayne Hamlin's rice farm is one of the biggest in the north state. His operation is vertically integrated from production to retail. His business includes rice exports to Japan. He owns a processing facility that designs and produces gluten-free foods to serve the growing demand of that market. His daughter successfully

operates an internet grocery store, specializing in gluten-free foods.

Wayne, 64, has been married to his wife Anne, 62, for 41 years. Anne has spent much of her adult life as a stay-at-home Mom. She helps out on the farm as necessary, primarily managing the business. Wayne and Anne have four children. Their oldest, Eric, 37, is a local dentist. Curt, 35, works on the farm. Katie, 25, is the creator and business manager of the online grocery store. Tom, 22, is a college student studying civil engineering.

It is during our second meeting, in which Wayne details the objectives of his estate and business succession plans. Wayne's objectives include:
1. Retain control yet plan for a gradual ownership transition to active children.
2. Reduce estate tax and transfer obligations.
3. Plan for contingencies such as death and disability.
4. Ensure equitable distributions of assets to all children.
5. Plan for continued spousal support.

While reviewing, the following business ownership transition tools from an estate planning perspective, pay attention to which alternative may or may not help Wayne achieve his objectives. Take a look at the simplified matrix below. It is designed to provide a quick reference tool. This tool may help you consider which concepts address the objectives most important in your estate plan.

Table 9-1. Estate Planning Concepts

Estate Planning Concept	Retain Control	Reduce Estate Tax and Transfer Obligations	Allow for Contingencies Such as Death/ Disability
Grantor-retained annuity trust (GRAT)	Yes, designed as a "grantor-retained" trust.	Yes, if you die following the term of the trust; no if during the term of the trust.	No, if you die during the terms of the trust; asset included in your estate.
Intentionally defective irrevocable trust (IDIT)	No, you retain control for income tax, not estate tax.	Yes, removes the farm/ agribus. from your estate.	Yes, asset is passed to the trust. No longer included in your estate. Note payment included in your estate.
Family limited partnership (FLP)	Yes, with gradual distribution of ownership or control.	Yes, removes large share of ownership interest from estate.	Yes, most of the shares of ownership are dispersed to your heirs as designed of FLP.
Private annuity	No, farm/ agribus. is sold	Yes, removes farm/agribus. from your estate.	Yes, the annuity payments cease upon your death.
Self-Canceling installment note (SCIN)	No, farm/ agribus. is sold	Yes, removes farm/agribus. from your estate.	Yes, the note is self-canceling upon your death.

Estate Planning Concept	Ensure Equitable Distribution	Continued Spousal Support
Grantor-retained annuity trust (GRAT)	No, though the trust can be distributed among active/passive children—not recommended.	No, at the conclusion of the terms of the trust, no inactive/passive income continues, and no asset is retained.
Intentionally defective irrevocable trust (IDIT)	No, though the trust can be distributed among active/passive children, not recommended.	Yes, as the nature of ongoing payments is a promissory note, the terms may be negotiated at inception.
Family limited partnership (FLP)	No, though the ownership shares can be distributed among active/passive children, not recommended.	Yes, ownership interest may be retained on which distributions are made.
Private annuity	No, though the ownership can be sold to active/passive children, not recommended.	No, unless annuity is written as a joint life annuity.
Self-Canceling installment note (SCIN)	No, though the ownership can be sold to active/passive children, not recommended.	No, self-canceling stipulation in note cancels upon your death.

PLANNING FOR ADEQUATE CAPITAL

Please do not discount the importance of ready cash for a complete estate plan. Ready cash is as important to estate planning as it is to the farm's success. One of the most important reasons that most farm/agribusinesses do not pass to the next generation is insufficient capital. "Money is honey," says a character in the play "The Producers." That is because almost everything costs money. Living costs money. Maintaining a business costs money. Even dying costs money. We have all heard the expression about death and taxes. It could be modified to death and financial obligations.

Your farm is probably the biggest asset in your estate. At times, as a business owner, you may get so focused on business development that you forget the vitality of retaining some ready capital for maintaining a successful business. In your drive to leverage your earnings, you may forget a rainy day fund. Other than a loan against the value of the business or the sale of the business, cash can be, at times, difficult to obtain. A business loan, though normally an option, is not readily available to a business during times of great distress. Distress can result from the death of the founder, chief executive officer (CEO), or a key employee.

Selling your business in an effort to convert assets to cash may happen in bad times. When does a business most need money? When production is down, sales are flat, expenses are up, or there is some calamity. Your untimely death may trigger a huge crisis for the business. Selling your business under less than ideal conditions will exacerbate an already terrible situation. The financial reality that comes from a distress sale always produces less than a fair return. The long-term effect of selling the family farm may be devastating. Family members may lose jobs, and the family most likely will never own that farm—or any farm—again.

PAY THE ESTATE TAX IN INSTALLMENTS

With the assumption that your primary asset is your farm, your family may elect to pay the estate tax in installments. Installment payments can be made over 14 years. The payments can be interest only for the first four years, then principal and interest for the remainder. Though this does not decrease the estate tax burden imposed on your estate, it does offer some planning opportunities.

Section 6166 of the Internal Revenue Code allows for a maximum of ten equal installments of principal and interest no later than five years after regular payment is due. The tax code allows installment payments under 6166 if the following conditions are met:

1. The owner of the closely held business interest (including sole proprietors, partners, or shareholders of a corporation) is included in the gross estate of a decedent at the time of death.
2. The business interest represents 35% or more of your adjusted gross estate.

The tax code applies an interest rate of 2% to the deferred estate tax directly attributable to the first $1.14 million dollars in taxable value that exceeds your applicable exclusion amount. Using the 2005 schedule, the tax applicable to your estate for the amount between $1.5 million and $2.64 million will be eligible for the 2% interest rate. Above the $1.14 million, the interest rate reverts to 45% of the rate applicable to underpayments of tax. The benefits of 6166 represent a planning tool that must be considered as you review your estate planning options.

Interest expense paid on deferred estate tax is not deductible.

A closely held business interest is specifically defined as follows in Section 6166 of the Internal Revenue Code:

1. An ownership interest as a proprietor in a proprietorship carrying on a trade or business.
2. An ownership interest as a partner in a partnership carrying on a trade or business if 20% or more of the total capital interest of the partnership is included in your gross estate, or if the partnership has no more than 45 partners.
3. Stock in a corporation carrying on a trade or business if 20% or more of the voting stock of the corporation is included in your gross estate, or the corporation has no more than 45 stockholders.

Though a limited liability company (LLC) is not specifically addressed in these definitions, you may assume that they apply to the LLC ownership model. From the Internal Revenue Code's perspective, LLCs are treated as partnerships, or corporations. Joint ventures are also viewed as partnerships in the tax code.

Known as the rules of attribution, ownership interest held by your spouse or close family members may be attributed to you. Note the following rules for further clarification:

1. Ownership shares held by a husband and wife are considered to have one owner if held as community property, joint tenants, tenants by the entirety, or tenants in common.
2. Stock and partnership interest owned by your

siblings, spouse, ancestors, or linear descendants will be considered your property.

3. Stock or a partnership interest owned by a corporation, partnership, estate, or trust is considered proportionately owned by the shareholders, partners, or beneficiaries not by the entity itself.

THE 35% TEST

Section 6166 specifically addresses the estate tax deferral that is available to the estate of a person who is either a resident of the United States or a citizen. The person's business interest must be 35% or more of the adjusted gross estate. As explained previously your gross estate is everything you own. Then one deducts funeral, administrative expenses, mortgages, debts, and claims against your estate and uninsured losses. In an effort to avoid deathbed planning, the Internal Revenue Service (IRS) will bring gifts made to others within three years of your death back into your estate.

INTERNAL REVENUE CODE SECTION 303

The corporate form of ownership may be a good way to hold title to your agribusiness. The corporate form of ownership provides some advantages in satisfying your estate tax obligation. We have discussed the estate tax obligation, the enormity of the need and the necessity for cash. If your family needs money to pay estate taxes, redeeming some corporate stock may be the solution. Under normal conditions, when a corporation buys stock back (redeems stock) from a shareholder, the proceeds are treated as a dividend distribution, and taxed as ordinary income. Internal Revenue Code Section 303 allows the redemption of the stock by the corporation to be treated as a sale. This subjects the proceeds to capital gains tax rather than ordinary income. Since stock is received following a distribution from an estate under the step-up basis rules, the gain on the stock will be little or not at all. This effectively allows a tax-free redemption of stock to satisfy the funeral expenses, administrative costs, and the estate tax.

SECTION 303 REDEMPTION

Section 303 redemption is available, no matter what class of stock a person may redeem. Common, preferred, voting, or nonvoting stock all qualify for redemption under section 303 of the Internal Revenue Code.

To qualify for Section 303 redemption, the value of redeeming corporate stock, included in your estate, must exceed 35% of your adjusted gross estate. Recall your adjusted gross estate is your gross estate less funeral expenses, outstanding debts, and uninsured casualty losses. The following example may clarify the 35% test:

Case Study

Robert owned only 5% of his family's (second generation) soil conditioning business. The estimated value of his interest at the time of his death was $550,000. His other assets were valued at approximately $2.1 million for a gross estate of $2.65 million. After subtracting the cost for funeral expenses and outstanding debts, Robert had an adjusted gross estate of $1.5 million. His corporate interest is 37% of his adjusted gross estate ($550,000 divided by his adjusted gross estate of $1.5 million).

The primary focus of the 35% test is the value of corporate stock in relation to your adjusted gross estate. Note that the percentage of the corporate stock that you own does not matter. It is the value of stock you own in relation to your estate.

You may combine the value of two separate corporations to meet the 35% if you own at least 20% of a single corporation. Combining the value of two corporations to meet the 35% percent ownership does make a difference.

AMOUNT ELIGIBLE FOR REDEMPTION

The amount of stock eligible for redemption, under section 303, is limited to estate taxes, funeral costs, and administrative expenses. The redemption must occur between the date of death and three years and nine months after the due date of the estate tax return.

SPECIAL USE VALUATION

Special use valuation (Internal Revenue Code Section 2032A) is another tax law designed to help farmers. This law states that real estate normally used in a farm operation may be valued, for estate tax purposes, at its actual value rather than its highest and best use. For example, if your farm/ranch is located in an area with major development pressures, the land may be worth more to a developer for its subdivision potential than to your heirs as a working farm. If the government could tax your property for its highest and best use, subdivision potential in this example, the value assessed may significantly increase the value of your property for estate tax purposes. This special use valuation allows for reductions in your gross estate of up to $840,000 (for 2003).

A few of the stipulations that apply directly to this special use valuation law include the following.

1. The property must be in the United States.
2. It must be used in a farm, trade, or business on the date of death.
3. The adjusted value of the real and personal property used in the farm or business enterprise must constitute at least 50% of the decedent's gross estate
4. The decedent must have been directly involved in the farming operation for at least five of the last eight years prior to death.
5. Finally, the qualified heir must maintain ownership of the property for at least 10 years following the decedent's date of death or pay substantial tax penalties.

COMMON ESTATE PLANNING MISTAKES

There are plenty of books on the subject of estate planning. Although involving law, accounting and insurance, estate planning is still more art than science. The 'art' is in the creation of an effective estate plan that –

1. Fits your situation.
2. Addresses your concerns.
3. Acts as a proxy carrying out your intentions.
4. Demonstrates love for your family through the legacy you leave.

The power of denial is a detriment to sound estate planning. Although it is hard to face your own mortality, you have an obligation to those you truly love to be prepared for the "when" and not procrastinate with the "if." The following common mistakes can be detrimental to a family when settling an estate planning.

Wills should not be invalid, out-of-date, or poorly written. This first point is self-explanatory. If a will is the foun-dation of your estate plan, it must be well-written, complete, legal, and up-to-date.

Wills should not be simple wills ("I love you" wills). A will leaving everything to your spouse, though better than no will at all, is inefficient and tax irresponsible. If you take the time and spend the money to write a will, do it right. Include provisions for a testamentary credit shelter trust.

You should have adequate life insurance coverage and proper ownership or appropriate beneficiaries. Life insurance included in your estate with improper ownership or beneficiary designation may compound your estate tax problem. Though some coverage is better than none, life insurance is relatively inexpensive when weighed against the benefit.

Improper or poorly planned property ownership is a common pitfall. A property not titled correctly or ina-ppropriately for the stipulations of the will or trust, only will confuse and frustrate the efforts of your executor and your beneficiaries. A large part of estate planning is making sure you use a consistent approach in the many facets of your estate plan.

Inadequate capitalization will not satisfy estate taxes, administrative expenses and transfer obligations. Most farmers are land rich and cash poor. Providing adequate liquid capital could be the difference between passing your farm to the next generation and complete liquidation.

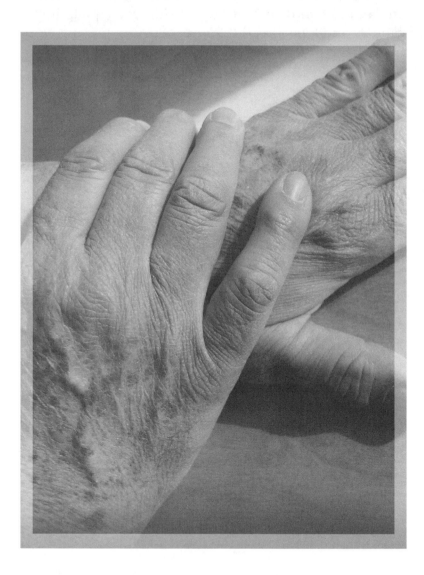

part 4
RETIREMENT
PLANNING

This section is not designed to teach investment strategies or to convince you to invest in the stock market. The goal is to teach you simple retirement planning strategies, which are designed to help you with the succession planning process.

Retirement planning, or the next venture in your vocational life, is about acquiring and maintaining financial independence. Financial independence means that you have earned and saved enough money to satisfy your ongoing financial needs, that you are able to increase your wealth over a 20 to 30 year retirement, and that you can satisfy the objectives of your intended bequests.

chapter 10
RETIREMENT PLANNING

Positioning yourself to realize financial independence is up to you, no matter what the goal may be. Retirement planning is the means by which you reach your goal. Retirement may include plans to build a subsidiary business, start an entirely new business in a related field, turn a hobby into a business, get a job in town, or coach football at the local junior college as a volunteer assistant. Articulating a dream that fuels your passion, applying a monetary value with a specific time frame for its accomplishment, and then taking the action necessary to bring your dream to fruition encompass retirement planning and financial independence.

With life spans quickly approaching the nineties and with continued improvements in physical health and fitness, your skills and talents could possibly be in demand as long as you are able and willing to work. Your biggest challenge may be to determine where to invest your talents and your expertise. Demand for the person who can tackle a problem from start to finish, accept uncertainty, work with ambiguity, and understand the risk inherent in new ventures, will always be more than the population can fill.

Farmers are the world's true entrepreneurs. You work through growing season after growing season, start to finish, under the premise that if the crop comes in, if the demand is high enough, and if the weather cooperates, you may profit. There will always be a demand for people who work hard, finish a job, and make a real contribution.

RETIREMENT PLANNING

A business owner has two sources of retirement income. The first is the money the business generates as a result of a sale of the business (equity), and the second is the savings and investments (retirement plans and investments) set aside through the years. Farmers not unlike most business owners can use any type of retirement plan. If you are a corporation, a profit-sharing or defined benefit plan may be appropriate. If you are a sole proprietor, a simplified employee pension plan, individual retirement account, or Keogh plan may be what you need. A 401(k) can be offered if employees are involved.

Depending on the sale of the farm as the source of retirement income is like placing a bet at the horse track. The first assumption must be that the farm will be sold and not passed to the next generation. In addition, you must be able to pick the right timing, the right economic conditions, and the right price.

- What if the farm is not successful, even with the best intentions and dedication operations fail?
- What if the timing is not right? Succession, especially when a sale is involved, is complicated. It takes time, patience, and, of course, the right buyer.
- What if the net financial result is inadequate to fund your retirement plans? Will the net proceeds from the sale adequately fund a 20 to 30 year retirement?

- What if your successor is unprepared or plans inappropriately to assume the leadership role? If the success of the operation is owner-dependent, how will a change in ownership affect the continued success of the operation?

FOUR VARIABLES THAT AFFECT RETIREMENT PLANNING

Four variables determine the success or failure of every retirement plan.

Contribution Amount How much money is being invested to fund the retirement plan? Should more money be contributed or can you contribute less and still satisfy your retirement objective? Is there a realistic factor for inflation considered in the accumulation goal?

Time Do you have enough time to reach the accumulation goal? Should you extend the time allotted for you to reach your goal or can it be shortened? Compound interest can have a profound effect in later years.

Return On Investment Considering the interest earned, dividends reinvested, and capital appreciation, is the rate of return optimal for the given level of risk? Should you consider accepting more risk in an effort to increase returns? How your earnings are taxed also plays an important part in your investment selection.

Accumulation Goal Is the goal attainable given the other three variables? Should the goal be changed based on the positive or negative effects of the other three variables? Would you realize more money from the sale of your farm than originally planned?

CALCULATE YOUR RETIREMENT NEEDS

Use a sheet of scratch paper and perform this simple retirement calculation. You may be surprised by your answers. Many people are overwhelmed if the shortfall seems insurmountable. A very few are elated that they have done so well. Retirement planning begins with a reality check. How much will it cost to satisfy your retirement needs financially? To accomplish the goal of financial independence, you must know your target.

The following table allows you to calculate monthly expenses after you leave the farm. Figure out how many dollars are needed to meet monthly retirement expenses satisfactorily. Some costs decrease after retirement such as costs related to work clothing and equipment repair. Other costs increase such as travel, entertainment, housing, and medical expenses. In the appropriate space below, record your current expenses and your projected retirement expenses. Use monthly expenses and multiply by 12 for a total that represents estimated annual retirement expenses.

Table 10-1. Cash Needs at Retirement

		Current Expenses	Retirement Expenses
Housing	Mortgage payment		
	Utilities		
	Housing maintenance		
	Property insurance		
	Property taxes		

	Home furnishings		
Food and household expenses	Groceries		
	Household supplies		
Clothing	Clothing purchases		
	Cleaning		
Transportation	Automobile payments		
	Automobile insurance		
	Fuel, repairs, and parking		
Insurance (not property)	Health insurance		
	Life insurance		
	Liability insurance		
	Long-term care insurance		
Entertainment and recreation	Vacation and travel		
	Meals and other entertainment		
	Clubs and recreation		
Charitable contributions			
Debt repayment (not housing and automobile)	Credit card debt and outstanding bills		

	Installment notes		
	Rental or investment property		
	Other debt		
Miscellaneous expenses	Education		
	Gifts		
	Domestic help or landscaping		
	Alimony or child support		
	Professional expenses		
	Other		
Total Expenditures			

DEVASTATING EFFECTS OF INFLATION

Inflation is to a retirement plan as rust is to unprotected farm equipment. From one year to the next, the erosive consequence is barely discernable, but over time, rust can completely destroy any vulnerable equipment. Take a snapshot today of an exposed implement in the farmyard. Ten years from now compare the snapshot with the same piece of equipment. The difference will be startling. The paint is fading, and rust is attacking the exposed metal. Over a 20-year period, you may not recognize a likeness to the original implement. Likewise, a retirement savings plan unprotected from the corrosive effects of inflation erodes the purchasing power of your retirement savings over time. The reality of your retirement is nowhere near the mental image you have envisioned.

Still need convincing? Consider a first-class postage stamp. In 1975, a mere 30 years ago, first-class postage was $0.10. Today that same first-class postage is $0.39. Inflation has caused the cost to increase nearly four times over the last 30 years. Some costs have increased at less than the normal 3.1%. Other costs, such as medical costs, have escalated at rates significantly higher than the 3.1%. With retirement often covering 20 to 30 years, inflation must be factored into retirement projections.

Now calculate your retirement income. Primary sources, other than the sale of the farm, might include:

1. Second deeds of trust
2. Employer-sponsored retirement plans
3. Individual Retirement Accounts (IRAs)
4. Keogh plans,
5. SEP IRAs
6. Social Security
7. personal savings

Table 10-2. Income at Retirement

		Current Income	Retirement Income
Earned income	Husband		
	Wife		

Retirement plant/IRA distributions	Husband		
	Wife		
Social Security benefits	Husband		
	Wife		
Interest income			
Dividend income			
Royalty income	Husband		
	Wife		
Consultation income	Husband		
	Wife		
Other distributions			
Cash receipts	Sale of assets		
	Alimony or child support		
	Trust distributions		
	Other		
Total cash receipts			

As you review all of the sources of retirement income, identify all of the known variables that may create restrictive conditions or time limits, such as payout periods, tax consequences, required distributions, and fees. The income you are trying to identify is relatively predictable.

Calculate the amount of money you need for retirement. View financial goals, especially related to retirement, as debt in your future that must be satisfied. As you complete this calculation, recall the four variables that drive every savings and investment plan: the contribution amount, time, returns on investment, and accumulation goal. Changing one or more of these variables impacts the outcome of your investment plan. Even a conservative investor may have to consider greater risk if the shortfall is too large. The intention of your plan is to save for retirement not to beat the stock market.

Table 10-3. Retirement Excess or Deficit		
Total cash receipts (above)	$	
Total expenditures (above)	$	
Retirement deficit: Expenditures exceed receipts. Plan to offset deficit? Invest more? Accept more volatility or decrease retirement expenditures.	-$	
Retirement excess: Receipts exceed expenditures. Plan to invest excess to offset devastating affects of inflation?		+$

LONGER LIFE SPANS MEANS
LONGER RETIREMENTS

In the past, life was simpler. Most people did not do financial planning. The farmer of yesterday worked right up until his last days on this earth only to leave the farm and all his worldly possessions to a son or a wife. Today, conditions are different. Medical science and healthy lifestyles have caused life expectancy to skyrocket. Today many people enjoy a retirement of 20 to 30 years.

Remember, back in 1965, the futurists of that time were predicting a population boom. They thought the earth would be overcrowded by the astounding number of births. The population explosion in this country, prompted by the postwar baby boom, caused quite a stir. At that time no one foresaw the phenomenon at the other end of the age spectrum. The population boom is not caused by too many kids – it is, instead, a direct result of longer life expectancies. How many times have you heard the tongue-in-cheek expression, "If I knew I was going to live this long, I would have taken better care of myself"? Rephrasing that expression to, "If I knew I was going to live this long, I would have better prepared for my retirement" may be more applicable today. The elderly population is the single fastest growing segment of the U.S. population.

According to the U.S. Census Bureau, by the year 2035, approximately 70 million people will be 65 years of age or older. The United Nations expects that by the year 2050, there will be nearly 2 billion people in their sixties, a number equal to the current populations of Europe, North America, and India combined. At the same time, while populations are living longer, the workforce population is declining at an alarming rate.

Thus, in order to achieve financial independence, people are going to have to invest outside their comfort zone. Some money should be invested off the farm into a diversified set of worthwhile investments. Risk is a factor in everyday life and it is certainly inherent in the farming lifestyle. Agribusiness is a business where you exercise little, if any, control over the circumstances of your environment. Planting, production, and harvest are timed against the weather. As an agribusiness owner, you bet on demand and commodity prices – months, sometimes years, before the harvest. Labor costs and other inputs of production are expensed, hoping for a positive return at harvest time. Everything about farming is a calculated risk until the crop is in and the check is received. Though investing off the farm may seem foreign, and even a bit chancy, it actually reduces some risk and diversifies your holdings.

RETIREMENT CALCULATORS

Investors who are reluctant to share details of their financial affairs with others may prefer the impersonal—and nonjudgmental—approach of a Web-based retirement calculator. Even simple retirement calculators can be useful because they perform sophisticated computations that most people cannot do on their own.

In theory, most retirement calculators are simple enough. You enter your age, salary, pension, current assets, and current investments. Next, you plug in how much of your salary you are saving, the age at which you would like to retire, and the income you would like to have in retirement. The retirement calculator typically supplies an estimate of your future Social Security benefits and then renders a verdict: yes, you are on the right track, or no, you will fall short.

DOING THE CALCULATIONS

First, decide how much money you need. Money is one of life's necessities. It provides security, represents opportunity, measures success, supports our standard of living, supplements our motivation, capitalizes our business ventures, allows us to leverage investments, and provides our standard of living. Everyone knows and readily admits that nothing replaces money. It is one of the fuels that fire the engines of life. Anyone who says money is not important has never gone without it!

Visualize buckets as the receptacles for your savings, retirement, emergency funds, college savings, and investments. Each bucket has a specific purpose, a dollar value, or an amount of money that constitutes a full bucket, and a time constraint. The aim becomes filling the buckets through earnings, investments, and equity appreciation.

The focus of this section is the retirement bucket. Begin with a specific retirement timeline. (Goals can always be adjusted over time, but they must be specific).

- How long do you have before you want to retire?
- How many more working years do you need?
- How many more growing seasons are needed?
- How much money are you going to need when you retire?

Case History

Assume for a moment that you are a young farmer with $50,000 accumulated in your retirement bucket. Considering your financial resources, you have calculated a capital shortfall of $300,000 to achieve your retirement needs. Your timeline is to 20 years. A 10% total return based on historical performance has become the standard financial gauge for most investors, but total return is nothing more than a visual display of the past and only certain aspects of the past at that. It is not an indicator of future performance. Historical perfor-mance tells only a fraction of the story and can be very misleading, but unfortunately, it is the only indicator.

A dollar goal projection illustrates the magic of compounding, using the historical rate of return. At a 10% return, your $50,000 investment grows to $336,000 in 20 years, and a whopping $872,000 in 30 years. However, there is a danger in not looking at the whole picture. Total return, $336,000 in 20 years or $872,000 in 30 years, drastically overstates the purchasing power that you will have because it ignores taxes, fees, and inflation. In any combination, these three asset eroders can have devastating effects on your expected return.

What a difference an oversight like this can make! With typical taxes of 2.5% plus fees, the 10% return is quickly reduced to 5%. So after taxes and fees, $50,000 in 20 years is not worth $336,000, but only $132,000. Subtract 3% for inflation, and real dollar projections drop to $74,000. Whoops! You discover that you will not hit your target! In fact, you could be off by hundreds of thousands of dollars and not have the time to make it up. This creates a frustrated investor who becomes, in effect, a market timer—often selling an existing fund and buying a new one in hopes of gaining back lost ground. The classic buy-high, selllow syndrome is the reason so many farmers hate the stock market. They try investing a few times and become disillusioned with the never-ending process of picking new actively managed investments only to be disillusioned by dismal returns and seemingly empty promises.

Your goal should be to focus on the total after-tax return you need. Total after-tax return is after fees, after expenses, after anything and everything that stands in the way of you falling short of your goal.

Use Table 10-1, 10-2, and 10-3 to project monthly retirement expenses, calculate an income, and then extrapolate a shortfall. A shortfall is the difference between what is realistically needed and what you project as available. It is the difference between anticipated income and projected earnings.

THE BEST CALCULATORS

American Savings Education Council (Asec). The simplest retirement calculator of all may be "Ballpark Estimate," a planning tool developed by the nonprofit ASEC. It is designed to provide a rough estimate of what you will need to save each year to fund a comfortable retirement. The ASEC's "Ballpark Estimate" worksheet is part of the free "Financial Facts Tool Kit" developed by the Securities and Exchange Commission. You can get a copy at www. sec.gov/investor/pubs/toolkit.htm or by calling (800) 732-0330. The ASEC offers more than a dozen other retirement calculators at www.choosetosave.org/tools/ fincalcs.htm.

American Association Of Retired Persons (Aarp). You can find the AARP retirement calculator at www.aarp.org/bulletin (click on "Online retirement calculator").

Quicken Retirement Calculator. USA Today calls the Quicken Retirement Calculator the "Cadillac of retirement calculators," partly because it factors in your tax rate after retirement: www.quicken.com/retirement/planner.

MENTAL ACCOUNTING

Mental accounting is the process of compartmentalizing your investments. It means mentally placing certain pools of money into different categories. This is something most people do automatically without much thought. For instance, imagine that you have a closet full of clothes; you place your "going out" clothes in one area and your work clothes in another. Then you compartmentalize your "going out" clothes into casual and dressy. You may or may not have physically partitioned your clothes; however, in your mind you have almost certainly placed certain items into each category.

We do the same thing with money; however, most people do not have a rational way of structuring mental compartments for their money. This type of thinking ends up in a hodgepodge of savings and investments, and you will not have a disciplined way to examine opportunities or scrutinize problems as they arise. Most people find themselves disorganized, unprepared, and even worse, making critical mistakes that can be easily avoided.

For example, many farmers keep a portion of their "just in case" money in the bank while they borrow on their production lines or credit cards. If you do this, you are borrowing money at a very high interest rate (the average credit card charges 16% interest) and then lending it to the bank at a much lower one (about 3%). You are actually paying 10% a year for every dollar you have in CDs that is equal to what you owe in credit cards. This does not include the fact that you have to pay taxes on your CD return and will not receive any tax break on your credit card debt. The end result? The banks do well, but you do not.

I recommend that you do the mental compartment test, and then put your answers on paper where you can divide your money into three major "buckets": short-term, mid-term, long-term. These components have their own unique timeline. This will determine the risk you can take and which investments are appropriate for each component.

SHORT-TERM MONEY

Short-term money is incidental or everyday money. It is money you need for farm operations to pay bills, repair equipment, or buy seed. Short-term money needs to be absolutely zero risk because you are going to need it now or in the near future. The timeline for this money is typically the present to 18 months.

MID-TERM MONEY

Mid-term money is that used for major purchases, including buying a new tractor, paying for a son or daughter's wedding, and major medical expenses. For most major purchases, the timeline is 18 months to 5 years.

LONG-TERM MONEY

Long-term money is retirement money. What do you have set up for retirement? Even if retirement is not in your future, how will you fund the next venture in your vocational life? Everyone needs long-term money, even those people who have already retired. The typical timeline is five years to an indefinite period.

LIFE SITUATION: WHAT STAGE ARE YOU IN?

The proportionate mix of short-term, mid-term, and long-term money depends on the stage of life in which you are. Most people are never clearly in any one stage; rather they gradually progress through the stages as age and wealth dictate.

ACCUMULATION STAGE

The age range of this stage is usually 25 to 45 years. At this stage, a person is primarily in their earning and spending period. They have a lot of short-term money that is being earned and spent. Priorities are mostly goal-oriented or mid-term in nature. Money may be used for the children's education, paying off the farm, life and disability insurance, and, if possible, investments for future financial independence. Long-term assets are typically either non-diversified, with farm equity the largest asset, or inaccessible to a retirement plan. With a long timeline, you can target high-return, high-risk capital gain-oriented investments with your long-term money. You should be pouring as much as you can into your long-term bucket since, with time on your side,

Table 10-4. How to Have a Million Dollars at Age 65			
Amount You Have to Invest Each Month			
Starting Age	8% Return	10% Return	15% Return
25	$310	$180	$45
30	$470	$300	$90
35	$710	$490	$180
40	$1,100	$810	$370
45	$1,760	$1,390	$760
50	$2,960	$2,500	$1,640
55	$5,550	$5,000	$3,850
60	$13,700	$13,050	$11,600

every dollar can grow significantly. If you are young, it is not going to take a lot of capital to build a substantial retirement account. The chart below shows your starting ages, rates of return you would need, and the amount you would have to invest to have a million dollars at retirement. It's not impossible!

CONSOLIDATION PHASE

The age range is usually 45 to 65 years of age. The consolidation or mid-to-late-career stage of the typical life cycle is characterized by the period when income exceeds expenses, typically, after children have left home. Short-term income often exceeds needs; mid-term goals are diminished somewhat, and retirement planning becomes your primary goal.

This stage is characterized by the accumulation and growth of an investment portfolio. Farm equity and retirement plan benefits are becoming substantial as well. The timeline to retirement and beyond is still relatively long (10 to 20 years). At this stage earnings are typically maximized so there is very little need for additional short-term saving. Mid-term money serves certain goals and peace of mind. Long-term savings should become a major component of your asset mix.

SPENDING PHASE

The age range is usually 60 to 80 years of age. The "spending phase" is defined as the period when one is financially independent: that is, living expenses are covered not from earned income but from accumulated assets such as investments and retirement programs. There is a heavy reliance on personal investments and a focus on assets with relatively secure values, with more emphasis on dividends, interest, and rental income. Of course, your timeline may still be well over 20 or even 30 years, so some investments in your portfolio should continue to have growth and inflation-hedge potential.

GIFTING PHASE

The final life cycle stage of gifting occurs when the farmer comes to realize that he has more assets than he will ever need for personal spending and security. Your asset mix may not be different from the previous stage, but attitudes about the purpose of your investments change.

Short-term   Mid-term   Long-term

HOW MUCH MONEY WILL YOU NEED?

Recall the three buckets; you have the short-term bucket, mid-term bucket, long-term bucket. Examine your own investment mix or how much money you have allocated to each of these buckets? Is that amount consistent with your stage of life? Maybe some adjustments need to be made.

For the most part, farmers who have amassed significant wealth have done it by reinvesting most of their earnings back into the farm, equipment, or inputs of production. Your farming enterprise dominates the net worth figure on your balance sheet. For most farmers, the value of the farming operation constitutes 75% to 100% of your net worth. Once you achieve this, you have succeeded by sheer will and the horsepower of your tenacity. The trick now is to dismount from this horse and put on a younger rider while maintaining the momentum of a progressive operation.

PREPARING FOR TRANSITION

Questions to ask yourself at this point include the following:

- As I confront my own retirement, what is the

risk associated with a portfolio comprised of one asset class?

- Should I consider diversifying my financial interests now?
- Do I have strategies that transcend the risks of having wealth concentrated in one asset class?

Now, moving forward to the sale of your agribusiness, either to an independent third party or a family member, you are faced with some new problems: What am I going to do with all this money? How can I make it last? Where should it be invested?

WHAT COMES NEXT?

While most agribusiness owners will not receive the entire value of a business in one lump sum, you may receive large chunks of money at specific intervals over the next several years. You could be one of the few who receives all cash, pays your taxes, and can stick the money in the bank. There are as many different scenarios as there are owners. The value of this section is learning how to retain control of the investment without the need to become a financial expert.

When people prepare to retire, they are advised to project a cash flow from assets for about 30 years. For example, when a farmer sells the farm for a net lump sum after taxes of $1.5 million dollars, he might assume that he can find a risk-free investment that will generate $100,000 of annual income. However, after a few inquiries at the bank and discussions with informed friends, he discovers that he cannot get this return. He then realizes that nothing yields enough to generate that kind income consistently. Even good quality bonds today yield less than 2% to 3%, which means you would need to invest around $5 million to generate $100,000 a year.

Most farmers shy away from the stock market. It is not that they do not understand equities, they just hate the idea of giving up control to a stranger. The stock market seems too dependent on other people and circumstances– a dependence that is contrary to the typical farmer's nature. The choice becomes: do it yourself or get help from an advisor. Most people do want the advice of an expert and yet still remain in control.

SOURCES OF RETIREMENT INCOME

Retirement income is derived primarily from three sources: Social Security, qualified retirement plans, and individual savings/investments.

SOCIAL SECURITY

Social security was never intended to fully fund a person's retirement. It was originally designed to augment or provide a portion of an individual's retirement income. For an employee born before 1937, retirement age is 65. The retirement age increases for those born in 1960 or later to 67 years of age. For most farmers, retirement age is when, "I'm ready, and I don't plan on receiving much from Social Security."

Social security benefits are based on wages paid and reported over an employees working life. Up to 85% of a retiree's benefit can be taxed as ordinary income, but Social Security benefits are adjusted annually for inflation.

QUALIFIED RETIREMENT PLANS

"Qualified" is a term used to define a retirement plan that meets certain requirements or constraints dictated by laws of the federal government. Generally, qualified plans allow an employer or employee to contribute to the plan on a tax-deductible basis. Earnings within the plan are tax deferred until benefits are paid out as retirement income. Mandatory distribution rules apply along with constraints regarding contributions and penalties for early withdrawals.

EMPLOYER-SPONSORED QUALIFIED RETIREMENT PLANS

Employer-sponsored qualified retirement plans should be a consideration of every employer for the benefit of long-time employees as well as the employer's own financial security. Qualified plans can be established on an employer-sponsored basis or an individual basis. Employer-sponsored plans can be further categorized as defined benefit or defined contribution. Defined benefit plans specify the retirement benefit a person will receive. Most employers do not offer defined benefit plans due to the investment risk assumed by the employer. Defined benefit plans promise a specific benefit as opposed to a specific contribution. Examples might include 401(k), SEP IRAs, and SIMPLE IRAs. Employers promise to contribute a percentage of your salary into a retirement benefit plan. In a defined contribution plan, the investment risk is born by the participant, not by the employer. The investment in a defined benefit plan is dependent on all the investment variables such as contribution amount, time, return, and accumulation goal that affect all investments.

INDIVIDUAL QUALIFIED PLANS

Individual qualified plans should be considered for anyone planning to retire. Each person or family has distinctive needs that should be addressed. Tax qualified plans such as traditional IRAs and Roth IRAs allow a person to tailor their retirement investment plans to suit their specific needs. The benefits of an IRA plan may vary, depending on your situation, but the opportunity to ensure an adequate retirement for yourself and your family does exist. Advanced planning may very well be the difference between financial independence and dependence.

NONQUALIFIED PLANS

Non-qualified plans, such as deferred compensation, do not qualify for tax benefits. These plans are often used to provide additional benefits to key employees and executives. They may also be used as a tool in your succession planning.

INDIVIDUAL SAVINGS/INVESTMENTS

A person is encouraged to save and invest in any of a variety of investment vehicles. It is prudent to accumulate money for retirement in the form of an emergency fund, an investment source, or a pool of capital. The key to success with any investment rests on a person's ability to cope with personal emotions while facing the cyclical character of the respective market. Your investment skill, financial experiences, and risk tolerance all play an important role in your long-term financial success. Some of the areas you may consider when looking for individual investment opportunities include:

- Savings accounts, regular pass book accounts, money markets, certificates of deposit, and credit unions.
- Stocks, proportional ownership shares in America's great corporations.
- Bonds, including corporate, government, and municipal. Bonds constitute loans to the respective entity.
- Real estate, of which most farmers own plenty. Real estate is an excellent investment. Most farmers should consider other categories of investment to diversify their holdings.
- Annuities, which provide a safe savings plan for many investors.

OTHER SOURCES OF RETIREMENT INCOME

As a self-employed individual, a farmer can continue to work. If a vocation is particularly enjoyable or rewarding, you should consider the option of carrying on. In addition, business equity is a very important consideration in the retirement equation. An agribusiness owner should seek to reduce risk by thinking of his business equity as just one asset in his portfolio and then diversifying with other investment vehicles.

WHY THE STOCK MARKET?

The stock market represents an open market for the

purchase of proportional ownership shares in America's most successful business entities. The market, unlike any other type of investment available to the consumer, offers many positive features when considering retirement

> ### Case Study
>
> Imagine that an investor purchases shares valued at $1,000,000 in this particular mutual fund in January of 1973. Without any additional investment, he withdraws $60,000 a year (adjusted for inflation) until the year 2000. The investor realizes an inflation-adjusted income totaling $2,575,855 over the 27-year period. The year 2000 income alone is $133,277. The investor will pass to the family $1,470,818 at the end of the 27-year period. The total benefit from this single investment is $4,046,673.

and multigenerational wealth. Table 10-5 demonstrates the compounding value of dividends and appreciation realized in a mutual fund investment. This particular fund is Massachusetts Investors Trust, founded in 1924. The stated objective is to provide reasonable current income and long-term growth. The illustration begins in 1973 and includes the second worst bear (down) market since the Great Depression in the 1930s.

ADVICE PEOPLE WILL USE

A recent study conducted by Dalbar, a highly regarded financial research company, found that there are four types of advice people will use: personal financial advisors, electronic advisors, prepackaged advice, and guidance services.

One of the biggest challenges you face is differentiating good advice from bad advice. Personal financial advice is poorly defined for consumers, thus making it difficult to select a source. This problem is compounded by the entry of new players in the advice business. Unless you know enough to separate good advice from bad advice, you will likely lose faith in the entire advisor industry.

Key Point: Investor Profiles

- Nine in ten investors want advice for investments over $100,000.
- Investors do not really want a written financial plan. They prefer an advisor who is available, provides clear explanations of investment alternatives, and keeps them informed about the status of their investments.
- Investors value education over lower tax bills and high investment returns.
- Three in four people trust their advisor. One in four people distrust advisors because of the inherent conflict of interest associated with commissions and sales loads.
- Seventy percent of investors prefer paying a flat fee, or an asset-based charge, for advice.
- Eighty percent of consumers look to family and friends to find a financial advisor.
- Fifty-five percent of Americans view mutual fund companies as a reliable source of investment information.
- Seven in ten consumers, especially baby boomers, consider financial planners as the nation's most reliable providers of investment advice.

Table 10-1. Cash Needs at Retirement

Period End	Invest	Withdraw	Income	Capital	Reinvest	Market
01/01/73	$1,000,000	$ 0	$ 0	$ 0	0	$1,000,000
12/31/73		60,000	30,480	12,042	42,522	814,235
12/31/74		61,800	31,217	0	31,217	542,817
12/31/75		63,654	26,367	12,461	38,828	658,643
12/31/76		65,564	25,081	15,428	40,510	749,015
12/31/77		67,531	28,291	10,779	39,071	599,054
12/31/78		69,556	28,950	10,309	39,259	578,593
12/31/79		71,643	31,035	20,830	51,865	634,853
12/31/80		73,792	33,130	52,262	85,392	754,417
12/31/81		76,006	34,895	52,318	87,213	641,556
12/31/82		78,286	34,724	58,910	93,634	684,479
12/31/83		80,635	29,300	80,774	110,074	746,788
12/31/84		83,054	30,126	29,837	59,963	685,660
12/31/85		85,546	29,239	70,056	99,295	768,518
12/31/86		88,112	25,638	113,466	139,105	812,656
12/31/87		90,755	26,811	95,084	121,895	782,540
12/31/88		93,478	27,445	57,548	84,993	770,311

12/31/89		96,282	31,452	86,215	117,666	952,279
12/31/90		99,171	30,229	59,203	89,423	852,168
12/31/91		102,146	27,178	95,886	123,064	985,800
12/31/92		105,210	24,396	161,742	186,138	953,382
12/31/93		108,367	30,246	131,096	161,342	940,620
12/31/94		111,618	20,278	88,823	109,101	819,421
12/31/95		114,966	38,115	67,946	106,062	1,026,839
12/31/96		118,415	16,553	108,134	124,687	1,174,364
12/31/97		121,968	18,630	100,408	119,038	1,424,572
12/31/98		125,627	13,029	86,716	99,745	1,625,891
12/31/99		129,395	7,939	46,798	54,737	1,609,584
12/31/00		133,277	2,787	63,271	66,057	1,470,818
Total	$1,000,000	$2,575,855	$733,561	$1,788,342	$2,521,903	
Ending	balance					$1,470,818

(The New Financial Advisor, Nick Murray, 2001)

Dalbar has taken a step toward helping consumers understand the advice offerings available through a consumer
booklet, Advice Trust & Money. This booklet outlines
the four categories of advisory services available today,
and it compares the key features of each. Many advisors
distribute this booklet, and it is available at www.
DALBAR.com.

SIX STEPS TO FINANCIAL INDEPENDENCE

Larry Chambers, author of The First Time Investor, offers
a six-step process that will help you manage your
retirement. The six steps to financial independence are
simple. Combine the steps with the discipline necessary
to implement a plan, and you can reach your financial
goals. Ultimately, it is up to you and an advisor. If you
follow the steps, observing events within your control,
measuring your progress according to your goal, and
building an appropriate investment strategy, you can be
assured of the highest probability of success.

The focus of this process is on events that you can control.
You begin by determining a dollar goal to meet your
investment objectives at a point in the future. You
actually choose two goals—a target goal, what you would
optimally like to have, and a fallback goal, what you
actually need. Your financial goal can be viewed as a
future liability—money owed to the future you.

Next, you apply an investment strategy that has the highest
probability of achieving those results. The focus of your
attention is on the probability of achieving your long-term
financial goal (not the risk of a particular investment
strategy). You begin by adjusting the known variables
until you move as close to 100% probability of success

as possible.

Most people do not understand total returns or a time-weighted rate of return. Instead of thinking about rates of returns, consider terms of probabilities. Every kid who has ever played baseball understands probabilities and batting averages. Everyone understands his or her chances of winning a lottery. Relating to probabilities is simple and easy.

This discussion is often omitted from investment books because it is so simple. It requires gathering information about as many known variables of a particular investment as possible. Including your time frame, tax rates, investment/saving pools, 401(k), IRAs, taxable accounts, and future savings. Evaluate your current investment position compared to your long-term dollar needs. In most instances this evaluation indicates a shortfall.

The shortfall amount determines the risk you need to assume to reach your investment goals and accumulate the money you need. This is where you realize that it does not matter if you get the highest returns. Risk is an investment variable used in relationship to meeting your goals. It helps to determine your investment strategy.

From this starting point, you may want to work with a professional advisor to create a detailed allocation model, using your business equity as the major asset. For instance, you may augment your investment portfolio with an equity (stock) component that can be subdivided into large cap versus small cap, value versus growth, and domestic versus international. The critical step in this process is to optimize the allocation of investments between your taxable and tax-deferred portfolios. This becomes your long-term strategic investment plan with the highest statistical degree of probability of reaching your goals.

After this step is complete begin to research investment vehicles. The number of possible vehicles seems limitless. Each investment vehicle considered should go through an intensive qualitative and quantitative screening process. The process ensures that the investment complies with your stated investment objectives. The goal is to provide profitable results with a minimum of surprise. Investment vehicles should also be evaluated based on their tax ramifications.

STEP 1: CREATE INVESTOR-SPECIFIC FUTURE DOLLAR "OBLIGATION"

The information gathered should include everything that will have an effect on your real dollar needs, such as your estimated tax rate, Social Security benefits, retirement plan payouts, major financial transactions (sale of the business), budgeted obligations (such as college tuition), projected returns of the capital markets, and a factor for the impact of inflation on savings. This may sound complicated. By using reasonable estimates, it is possible to calculate reasonably accurate goals, although it is impossible to be 100% accurate. It is best to err on the conservative side. Assume the less desirable scenario, because it is better to end up with too much money than not enough.

Assume that you have gathered all of the information about your current financial situation. You have defined your financial goals. After some calculations of best- and worst-case scenario, you find that you have accumulated $1,400,000 in assets. After taxes, you compute that this will generate approximately a $90,000 annual income. On the conservative side, you calculate that you can still enjoy your retirement plans with a minimum of $40,000 in annual income or you need around $780,000 dollars in assets.

STEP 2: ADJUST DIVERSIFICATION MODEL

Table 10-6. Various Asset Classes in a Typical Portfolio

Asset Class	Risk	Expected Returns
Money market	Low	2.82%
One-year fixed	Low	3.77%
Five-year government	Low	4.17%
U. S. large company	High	10.66%
U. S. small company	High	12.85%
International large company	Higher	15.93%
International small company	Highest	16.68%
Model		**Expected Returns**
Defensive	Low	5.28%
Conservative	Moderate	8.63%
Moderate	High	10.40%
Aggressive	Highest	14.08%

Based on the assumptions made regarding your income needs in retirement and your current assets, adjust your diversification. You may require more growth or less risk. Your advisor can make some diversification recommendations, apportioning the investment portfolio by adding stocks, bonds, and cash. The asset mix for most agri-business owners is heavily weighted in real estate equity. Diversifying to other asset classes will dampen the volatility of a portfolio over time.

Returns are a function of a security's characteristics, business cycles, and investor behavior. Most investment professionals construct various allocation models. Stocks, for example, might be divided into model portfolios made up of large-cap value, large-cap growth, small-cap value, and international styles.

STEP 3: MEASURE AND REFINE THE OTHER ASSUMED VARIABLES

Investment success is not just predicated on optimizing the asset allocation to a goal. There are many variables that influence the outcome. Investor behavior and expectations are no small part of the success or failure of an investment plan. The probability of success is determined more by your behavior than any other factor in the investment equation. Realistic projections for time to success return assumptions, and systematic investment schedules must be built-in.

Assumed variables allow you to adjust your expectations according to current results. In case your actual results are not what they should be, you can adjust some variables—such as reduce expenses, increase your savings, and allocate more time to achieve your goals.

STEP 4: MINIMIZE THE TAX IMPACT

A critical step is tax liability management. Some focus must be placed on optimizing the allocation of investments between taxable and tax-deferred investments. Some investors and advisors become so myopic in their focus that they look at each pool of money on a stand-alone basis (i.e., IRA, 401(k), taxable savings). When investment objectives are not in concert with each other, an inefficient strategy on both an investment and tax basis is created. In this step, you work with your advisor or accountant with the goal of tax optimization. You want to use the correct investment style for the greatest comparative tax advantage.

STEP 5: EVALUATE POTENTIAL INVESTMENT VEHICLES

You have defined your dollar obligation, examined your diversification needs, confirmed your variable constraints, and planned to optimize your tax ramifications, now you need to evaluate potential investment vehicles to match your plan. There is an infinite number of potential investment vehicles, including private investment advisors, mutual funds, and indexed investments. Be sure your advisor goes through an extensive screening process before recommending an investment. The process should assure that you adhere to a stated discipline and specific objectives—providing quality results with few surprises.

STEP 6: CONSISTENTLY REVIEW PROGRESS TOWARD ACHIEVING YOUR GOALS

Once the plan is in place, you should consistently review your progress toward achieving your goals. Investment alternatives should adhere to the long-term objectives established in your investment plan. As the cyclic revolutions of the capital markets ebb and flow and the reality of multiple constraints temper your results, strategic changes may be necessary. Annually reviewing your progress allows you to adjust your strategy accordingly.

For instance, rebalancing may become necessary. There are three reasons to rebalance:
- Research indicates a change in return of a capital market
- If you have a change in circumstances
- If a tax code changes in a way that may adversely affect your results

Summary

Investing can be a daunting process. Pop financial advice, magazine articles, newspaper columns, trendy television shows, and infomercials are so pervasive today, and they all claim to have the cure-all regarding financial planning. Your financial security, your retirement, and your family's financial future all rely on you making correct decisions regarding your financial security. When all else fails, there are four absolutes by which you should abide to maximize your investment results and minimize the confusion inherent in the process.

The true long-term return of stocks is much greater than bonds. Investments with staid, secure returns can increase the risk of outliving your retirement income. You cannot successfully grow your investment to compensate for the eroding effects of inflation if your investment is not designed to grow. Bond returns are predicated on loaned money not invested money. As a loaner, you do not

---

Key Point: Investment Relations

- No one can consistently time the financial markets, that is, predict when it is appropriate to buy or sell. For that matter nobody can tell you which investment will show the greatest return over any given period of time.

- Diversify your investment portfolio. Mutual fund investments are like lifetime commitments, much like your investment in the farm. If you think in terms of a lifetime when selecting your mutual funds, you will make better decisions with your money. Selecting mutual funds based on a specific index or a competent money manager ensures real returns for the risk (volatility) you will realize.

- Investment results are not predicated as much on market behavior as on investor behavior. Do not be intimidated out of the market. Markets are volatile, investments fluctuate, but it is that fluctuation that fuels the return of equity mutual funds.

---

have an invested stake in the business; therefore you are not entitled to the returns of ownership.

part 5
UNDERSTANDING RISKS AND INVESTMENTS

An informed investor knows that all investments involve some element of risk. An increase in risk will signal an increase in return, or the potential reward. Understanding the types of investment risks and the ways that risk can be reduced is one of the most important pieces of information you need in completing your succession plan.

chapter 11
SIGNIFICANCE OF MONEY

Most people assume that financial planning is about making money. It is more about what money can do for you, specifically in regard to your standard of living, your business development, and the legacy you leave your family.

- What does "retirement" really mean to you and your family?
- Will you or your spouse work part-time?
- Will a current hobby become a valid source of income?
- Do you want to sell the farm and relocate?
- Do you want to travel?

Today people are redefining retirement. The days of retiring to a rocking chair on the front porch and living on a fixed income are over. Retirements lasting 20 to 30 years take a new level of thought and planning to achieve the goal of true financial independence.

MOVING FROM SUCCESS TO SIGNIFICANCE

Assuming you have achieved "financial success," is there more to financial success than retirement? Bob Buford, in his meaningful book, Half Time: Changing Your Game Plan from Success to Significance, notes: "One of the most common characteristics of a person nearing the end of the first half (of the game of life) is that unquenchable desire to move from success to significance."

Significance reflects the vision of your legacy after you transcend at death to a higher order where character means everything and net worth means nothing. A man of true depth recognizes that all earthly blessings are merely on loan to be left behind. Stewardship is the ideal that speaks directly to our responsibility to care for and nurture those blessings. Significance is a desire to give back during life and beyond death in order to make a difference.

- As you consider your responsibility as a steward, and the potential significance of your legacy, what are your heartfelt goals?
- Do you have charitable intentions?
- Do you wish to fund trusts, endow certain causes, build cultural edifices, create foundations, educate your grandchildren, and enlighten or in some way inspire others?

These are the soft, yet important, issues regarding money. Addressing these issues makes your investment program significant. The depth and breadth of the answers to these questions expose more complex meanings beyond money. Matters of significance require money, but money is not the point. Money serves as a means to an end, not the end in itself. The act of discovery and establishing goals means going beyond the data sheet. An in-depth understanding of core values and heartfelt financial objectives are initiated in face-to-face conversations over coffee, or at a meal in a relaxed atmosphere during unguarded moments. All too often we hide behind "paying the bills" and "getting by," while allowing our true wants and our passionate needs to go unaddressed.

Do you have trusts that own property? Living trusts or testamentary trusts from previous estate planning endeavors affect the disposition of your assets. Revocable or irrevocable trusts govern the distribution of your property.

Too many estate planning decisions are made based on minimizing estate taxes to the detriment of your own inheritance goals and the legacy you intend to leave. You have a responsibility, to yourself and your heirs, to have a working knowledge of your will, the impact of various forms of ownership, and a range of the contractual implications. You should feel comfortable with the uses of trusts. Learning about the vocabulary of trusts and the various options for their use is important to complete estate planning. Titling property correctly is not an idle query. In the interest of maintaining an effective succession plan, professional advice may be warranted any time a piece of property is bought or sold.

Estate and income tax ramifications may be significant. Tax issues have a tendency to misguide, and often control, rational thinking. Set aside the tax laws for a moment. Make believe that there are no ordinary income taxes, no capital gains taxes, and no estate taxes.

- How do you sincerely feel about your children as heirs? Are some of your heirs minors?
- If your heirs are adults, are there health issues, immaturity factors, special needs, or spendthrift concerns that you should consider?

The probability of greater longevity increases the likelihood of old age infirmities. The probability of living into your eighties and nineties places a greater emphasis on trust planning, both living trusts and testamentary (postmortem) trusts.

For a large estate, advanced estate planning strategies may be necessary. Life insurance continues to be a valuable tool to leverage your legacy. A cursory knowledge of advanced planning alternatives, combined with excellent professional coaching helps you to achieve your goals in the most efficient way possible.

CONCENTRATED WEALTH

Reinvesting earnings back into the farm operation, equipment, or inputs of production help most agribusiness owners to amass significant wealth. The farm enterprise comprises the biggest percentage of your net worth. For most agribusiness owners, the value of your farming operation constitutes 75% to 100% of your net worth. Your success is a result of the horsepower of your sheer will and tenacity. As mentioned previously, succession planning is about dismounting from this horse to put on a younger rider while maintaining the momentum of a progressive operation.

Several good questions to consider are as follows:

1. As I approach retirement, what is the risk of a portfolio comprised of one asset class?
2. Should I consider diversifying my financial interests now?

chapter 12
UNDERSTANDING RISKS AND INVESTMENTS

Strategies that transcend the risks associated with wealth concentrated in one asset class are increasingly important. Most people at sometime have been in an investment presentation in which the advisor uses the "investment pyramid" to explain risk. It is found in most investment books. It explains risk and return. "Safe investments," such as cash, are at the bottom. Mutual funds, real estate, investment trusts, and convertible bonds are in the middle, while individual stocks, venture capital, and commodities are at the top. It is easy to relate to this hierarchy and graphically visualize your money as safe or risky. You compartmentalize assets according to various levels of risk. However, when most people think of risk, they assume that risk is the likelihood of your investment losing value, but all securities are subject to various forms of risk.

- Increased risk of loss of capital
- Increased reward through appreciation

- Increased risk of loss of purchasing power
- Increased safety of principle

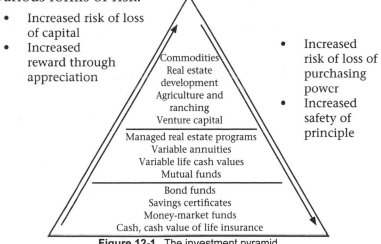

Commodities
Real estate development
Agriculture and ranching
Venture capital

Managed real estate programs
Variable annuities
Variable life cash values
Mutual funds

Bond funds
Savings certificates
Money-market funds
Cash, cash value of life insurance

Figure 12-1. The investment pyramid.

Risk Tolerance

Dalbar, a highly regarded financial research company, conducted a study entitled Quantitative Analysis of Investor Behavior (QAIB). The following table highlights the study's findings, which are astonishing facts about investor performance.

Table 12-1. Quantitative Analysis of Investor Behavior (QAIB)		
Category	Cumulative Return*	Annualized Return†
S&P 500 Index	793.34%	12.22%
Small Company Stock Index	538.94%	10.25%
Average Equity Fund Investor‡	**62.11%**	**2.57%**
Long-term Government Bond Index	718.05%	11.70%
Long-term Corporate Bond Index	659.30%	11.26%
Intermediate-term Bond Index	436.40%	9.24%
Average Fixed Income Fund (Bond) Investor	**120.06%**	**4.24%**
Treasury Bills	175.89%	5.49%
Inflation	79.80%	3.14%

*Calculated by Dalbar using data presented in Stocks, Bonds and Inflation 2003 Yearbook, Ibbotson & Associates, Inc. Based on copyrighted works by Ibbotson and Sinquefield. All rights reserved. Used with permission.
†Annualized return assumes returns are compounded annually.
‡The rate of return investors earn: based on the length of time shareholders actually remain invested in a fund and the historic performance of the fund's appropriate index.

How can it be that the Standard and Poor's 500 (S&P 500) has averaged 12.22% a year since 1984 yet the average equity investor averaged only 2.57%? According to Dalbar, the primary reason for this paltry performance is market timing. Instead of staying invested in the market, investors tend to pour more money into stocks after the market has performed well for short periods of time, essentially missing much of the upturn. True to form, investors tend to pull money out of the market after the decline and repeat this process time after time. In other words, they buy high and sell low.

The amount of return the average investor leaves on the table is shocking. The whole idea of investing in stocks is to beat bonds and inflation over time. However, look at the facts: the average bondholder actually beat the average equity investor by almost two to one, returning 4.24% (bondholders) versus 2.57% (stockholders). Sadly, inflation also beat the average equity investor.

People panic and go in and out of the market. This is the area where farmers make the biggest mistakes. They jump off the investment ship thinking it is sinking, when it really is not. Most people facing a significant downturn in their portfolio make shifts in an attempt to preserve equity. Thus, it is important that you know what your risk tolerance is so that you invest appropriately.

As a general rule when investing in stocks or other risky investments, you may experience twice the volatility as the expected rate of growth. What that means is if you are investing to capture 10% growth in a fully invested portfolio, you can expect to experience about twice that much in decline every three to five years. If you are looking for a 15% growth on a fully invested portfolio, you can expect declines in the range of 30% every three to five years. How do you know what to do?

Did you see the movie Titanic? Remember the scene after the iceberg hit the ship and worried passengers prepared to board the lifeboats? Some passengers were in a state of panic, while others did not seem to be upset until the ship was almost underwater. You can think of investment volatility in a similar way. When would you get in the lifeboat?

WHAT LEVEL OF DECLINE CAN YOU TOLERATE?

Assume for a moment that you have $100,000 invested in a retirement plan. Your monthly statement indicates that your $100,000 has dropped to $97,000. Can you stay on board for that? Then, the following month, your balance is down to $94,000, and subsequently it drops to $92,000. How are you feeling now? Are you still okay with doing nothing or are you getting your lifeboat ready? The month after that, it drops to $90,000. Then it goes down further: to $85,000, $77,000, $65,000, and eventually to $50,000. At what point did you jump into your lifeboat?

Most farmers do not care about relative performance; they care about absolute performance—what actually happens to their money. Take a look at the example below as a means by which to evaluate your own risk tolerance. Review the risk table and decide how much decline you could accept, both in dollar amounts and in percentages, before you feel compelled to jump. It is very important that you answer these questions honestly, as they will form the cornerstone of your investment strategy.

LIFEBOAT DRILL EXERCISE

Assume you have $200,000 invested in the stock market. On your next monthly statement, you see that your $200,000 has become $194,000. Are you still on board? The next month, you are down to $188,000, and then it drops to $184,000. How are you feeling now? Are you still okay with doing nothing, or are you getting your lifeboat ready? The month after that, it drops to $180,000, and then it drops to $170,000, $154,000, $130,000, and eventually to $100,000. At what point do you jump ship?

Table 12-2. Evaluate Your Own Risk Tolerance		
Potential Quarterly Decline	Original Investment $200,000	Check the box where you would take action
(3%)	$194,000	☐
(6%)	$188,000	☐
(8%)	$184,000	☐
(10%)	$180,000	☐
(15%)	$170,000	☐
(23%)	$154,000	☐
(35%)	$130,000	☐
(50%)	$100,000	☐

On your $200,000, you might be willing to endure a 3% decline, but you probably are not willing to sit still after a 5% drop. At a 15% drop, nearly everybody wants out. It interesting that most people are willing to accept a greater percentage amount when it is not related to a specific dollar amount. To demonstrate this, cover up the dollar amounts and repeat the exercise looking only at the percentages. Percentages are the financial service industry's equivalent of casino gambling chips. By abstracting money into chips or percentages, the impact of loss is lessened for the gambler and for the farmer.

YOUR TIMELINE AND RISK MANAGEMENT

Your time horizon is typically one of your investment constraints. Think in terms of how long until you need to use this money, viewed as three different timelines for investments.

TYPES OF RISK

Stock Market Risk

Stock market risk involves the threat that the securities you own will fluctuate because of changes in their price levels. Most people associate market risk only in relation to the stock market. Stock prices move up or down randomly. The financial health of a company is only a small part of the cause. Other securities are also subject to market risk. Bonds fluctuate according to changes in interest rates. Even bonds that are issued by the U. S. government, considered the safest investment, show volatility as interest rates change. When current interest rates go up, the prices of existing bonds go down. When interest rates go down, bond prices go up. Although, at maturity bonds are paid in full and the interest the bond pays does not change, bonds fluctuate in value over their terms.

General downturns in the business cycle can adversely affect specific investments. Watch the decrease in value of individual stocks when you see a drop in the Dow Jones Industrial Average. Many stocks suffer a decrease in value as a symptom of the overall market decrease. The drop in value is not necessarily tied to company-specific actions. Market shifts work both ways. An increase in the market may cause a corresponding increase in company values regardless of company performance.

You can reduce the effects of market risk by investing in short-term or fixed-principal securities (e.g., treasury bills, insured certificates of deposits, money market mutual funds, fixed annuities). Because of their low volatility, these securities tend to provide the lowest returns.

All investments depend on two factors: money to invest and time. Any threats to financial security may reduce or completely eliminate the flow of new income or deplete accumulated assets.

Reinvestment Risk

Reinvestment risk describes the possibility that your investment will yield less than you anticipated, hence your reinvested returns will not generate projected income. Most people are familiar with renewing a high-interest bank certificate of deposit only to find that the interest rate at renewal has dropped. Many investors make the mistake of seeking the comfort of stable non-fluctuating short-term investments, but the interest rates of these investments tend to be the lowest of all rates over time.

Liquidity Risk

Liquidity risk occurs when you need your money now.

It may come in the form of early withdrawal penalties or a low return due to a depressed market. The return on various investments may not be immediately available, could be subject to penalties, or you may have to accept a reduced market price. Liquidity is important if you need your money for unforeseen expenses or for an emergency. A familiar example of liquidity risk is the penalty that you incur if you take money out of a certificate of deposit before maturity. An early redemption from an annuity or other investment could be subject to an early withdrawal fee. (Some annuity back-out fees can be a high as 10%.)

Liquidity risk is reduced by investing in mutual funds and publicly traded securities that have a ready market. Mutual fund companies are legally required to redeem shares at the current net asset value on the day the fund company receives your redemption request. Consequently, they are considered liquid investments. Some funds may have redemption fees that are imposed if you redeem your shares within a prescribed amount of time.

Inflation Risk

Inflation risk is perhaps the most devastating menace. It affects all investments equally. Inflation could mean that your savings eventually will be inadequate for your retirement needs. Since the end of the Great Depression and the triumph of Keynesian economics, inflation has become an inherent part of the American economy. Today inflation runs at about 3% a year. Many people believe this level of inflation is acceptable, but this level is far higher than during other periods of economic growth.

Life expectancies are increasing. So it is likely that your retirement savings will have to provide you with income for 20 to 30 years. Your investments must return a minimum of 3% just to stay even with annual inflation. Factor in taxes and the fact that the economy is adversely affected by inflation, and you will need a much higher return just to afford the retirement you have set out to enjoy.

To combat inflation, you must have an investment program that has the potential of providing you with accreting capital and income. Unless your retirement savings continue to grow, you run the risk of receiving income with reduced purchasing power. That could mean a declining quality of your life.

Default Risk

Investments made in specific companies or organizations are subject to default risk. The potential for default due to poor management, economic cycles, or catastrophe presents a level of risk for any investment other than the U. S. government. Default risk can be minimized by purchasing investments in large, financially secure companies. However, this is no guarantee, but any discussion of investment risk assumes an offsetting reward for a consequent level of risk, including investment risk.

Interest-rate Risk

Interest-rate risk is the possibility that a fixed-interest investment incurs a decrease in market value due to a change in the prevailing interest rate. Bonds are particularly sensitive to changes in the interest rate. As interest rates increase, bond values decrease and vice versa.

Managing Risk

No one can foretell what will happen in the markets tomorrow, much less next week, next month, or next year. However, what you can do is blend markets to mitigate risk. There are five principles you can employ to smooth out market volatility: diversification, asset allocation, time, compounding, and rebalancing. These principles may dampen the roller-coaster ride associated with typical markets. Once you understand how these concepts work, you can use them.

PRINCIPLE 1: DIVERSIFICATION

The biggest mistake most people make is attempting to diversify within the same asset class. Diversification may be the most misused word in investment discussions. People often say, "I'm well diversified; I have my money in four mutual funds." However, these people are not really diversified if these four funds are all in the same asset class. This is why you should know what you are doing, or at least have an advisor who does.

Harry Markowitz, the Nobel Prize winner in economics in 1990, said "while almost all diversification is good, there is effective diversification and ineffective diversification." Simply put, if the separate components of your investment portfolio move up and down together, that is ineffective diversification. It is exactly the same as investing in one fund. There is likely a stock overlap in your funds.

A diversified portfolio provides stability and, hence, a larger long-term return, but only if you spread your money among asset classes that do not exhibit value fluctuations in the same direction at the same time (e.g., between value and growth funds, small and large cap funds, international growth and value funds). A diversified portfolio is comprised of many asset classes, some of which do well, and some of which do not do so well at any given time. Imagine a merry-go-round in an amusement park. Some horses are up while others are down. They are never all up or all down. Thus, the total return of a diversified portfolio is never as good as the current best asset class; nor is it ever as poor as the worst. However, the ride will be smoother, and the end result will be a superior return.

Investing in a portfolio that contains many securities of different companies will help you to avoid the risks associated with investing in securities of a few companies or companies in only one industry. The economy and the financial markets are ever-changing. Spreading your investments among many different companies in different industries can significantly reduce the risk of unpleasant surprises.

Diversification also means spreading your investments over different types of asset classes (e.g., bonds, stocks, short-term investments, and real estate). Each investment class has risks. Each fluctuates over time. Selecting diverse types of investments reduces the inherent risks of any one security type. The following story about an island economy exemplifies effective diversification.

Case Study

On Sovereignty Island there is a large resort and a manufacturing firm that makes umbrellas. Weather affects the fortunes of both businesses. During sunny seasons, the resort has a booming business, but umbrella sales plummet. During rainy seasons, the resort owner does poorly, while the umbrella manufacturer has strong sales and profits. The following table shows a hypothetical comparison of the earnings of the two businesses from season to season:

	Umbrella Manufacturer	Resort Owner
Rainy season	50%	-25%
Sunny season	-25%	50%

Suppose that, on average, one-half the seasons are sunny and one-half are rainy (i.e., the probability of a sunny or rainy season is 50%). An investor who bought stock in the umbrella manufacturer would find that half the time he earned a 50% return, and half the time he lost 25% of his investment. On average, he would earn a return of 12.5% if he earned 50% the first year and lost 25% the second. This is referred to as the investor's expected return. An investment in the resort produces the similar results. Investing in either one of these businesses would be more risky than investing in equal amounts of each.

Our investor puts half his money in the umbrella manufacturing business and half in the resort. Now, during the sunny seasons, a one-dollar investment in the resort would produce a 50-cent return, while a one-dollar investment in umbrella manufacturing would lose 25 cents. The investor's total return would be 25 cents (50 cents minus 25 cents), which is 12.5% of his total investment of two dollars.

The same thing happens during rainy seasons, except the payoff is realized in reverse. Investment in the umbrella company produces a 50% return, while the investment in the resort loses 25%. The advantage happens when there is a freak year. It rains all year or is sunny all year. If the investor owned shares in the resort, and it rained all year, he might have a 100% loss, but in our diversified model, the investor makes a 12.5% return on his total investment.

This illustration points out the advantage of diversification. Whatever happens to the weather, and thus to the island economy, by diversifying investments through two companies, an investor is making a 12.5% return each year. The principle that makes this work is that, while both companies are risky (returns are variable from season to season), the companies were affected differently by the weather's covariance. Covariance measures the degree by which two risky assets move in tandem. A positive covariance indicates that asset returns move together. A negative covariance means they vary inversely. As long as there is some lack of parallelism in the fortunes of the individual companies, diversification always reduces volatility of the overall investment.

Portfolios of volatile stocks might be put together in a similar way. The portfolio as a whole would actually be less risky than any one of the individual stocks in it. It is this negative covariance that plays the critical role in successful management of institutional stock portfolios. Negative covariance is one approach which helps to diversify the risks out of a portfolio.

DIVERSIFYING WITH EQUITIES

Figures from Chicago-based Ibbotson Associates showed that, from 1960 through 1985, farmland's compound annual total return was 11.9%. That was 3.2% better than the 8.7% return for the S&P 500 Index in the same period. The rate was achieved at less than half the stocks' standard deviation. Nevertheless, it is true this was before the bull stock market of the 1990s, in which the S&P average was over 10.5%. Does everyone remember what happened to farmland during the 1980s and early 1990s? That is when U. S. stocks went through the roof, and you could not give away farmland.

During those times when farmland was lagging stocks, you could have also owned a diversified portfolio of U. S equities (stocks). In this case, you would have enhanced your overall return while lowering your volatility. How is this possible?

The answer helped Harry Markowitz win a Nobel Prize in 1990 for the research he did in 1954. Back then, he wrote a 16-page doctoral dissertation that became known as Modern Portfolio Theory. Markowitz proved that, for a given expected return, reducing a portfolio's variance increases the compound rate of return. What that means is a negative covariance positively affects the return of an investment portfolio. This is what one investment researcher called an "asset class." If it has a low correlation with another asset class, then combining them can smooth out the ride and improve performance. In other words, since farmland and stocks do not move in tandem, a portfolio comprised of farmland and stocks may increase return while reducing volatility. This is why many smart people on Wall Street spend their time searching for asset classes that have a negative covariance or "low correlation."

What is low correlation? Correlation is a statistical measure of how the movements of two variables are related. Correlation measurements range from +1.00 (perfect positive correlation) to -1.00 (perfect negative correlation). When two assets have a +1.00 correlation, they move up and down in the same direction with the same magnitude. There is no diversification advantage to be gained by pairing two assets with a +1.00 correlation. On the other hand, pairing assets having a -1.00 correlation would be advantageous. The Ibbotson Associates' study showed that farmland and U. S. stocks had an almost perfect negative correlation with each other. Thus, the combined portfolio, of stocks and farmland, is less susceptible to volatility than individual assets. By owning farmland and owning a portfolio of stocks, you may have unintentionally constructed a sophisticated strategy. Modern Portfolio Theory also says you need to look at all of your investments as a whole not in isolation. The power of using correlation coefficients to construct well-diversified portfolios has been documented. The results are compelling.

The measurement of correlation and the utilization of asset classes with low correlation are fundamental ingredients of the modern investment theory. The principle of diversification offers greater comfort to the long-term investor because each kind of investment follows its own market cycle. Each asset responds differently to changes in the economy or the investment marketplace. If you own a variety of assets, a short-term decline in one asset class can be balanced by others that are stable or are experiencing a positive return. The key is to find groups of investment assets that do not move together. Instead look for assets that move inversely or opposite.

While some investors can tolerate the higher risk associated with not diversifying, most cannot. Suppose all your money was invested in farmland and you needed to sell some of your holdings for an emergency. If farmland prices were depressed at the time, you might be forced to take a loss on the sale. Owning other types of investments gives you more flexibility in raising the needed cash.

While money market funds provide liquidity and low risk, their overall return was 30% less for almost every 10-year period than the return from a diversified portfolio. That is a high price to pay for perceived investment stability. A diversified portfolio, on the other hand, provides both liquidity and comparative stability.

Diversification is a prudent method for managing certain types of investment risk. Unsystematic risks, such as management risks, competitive risks, and financial risks, can be reduced through diversification. However, this is not effective if all the assets are invested in the same market segment or in market segments that tend to move in tandem. If all investments were to decrease in value at the same time, that type of diversification would be ineffective. For instance, one could own a representative equivalent of the S&P 500 Stock Index, and the Dow Jones Industrial Average. Since both tend to move in the same direction at the same time, this would not be effective diversification.

While all diversification is good, certain types of diversification are better. This was the premise of Harry Markowitz's theory. He showed that to the extent that securities in a portfolio do not move in concert with each other, their individual risks can be effectively diversified away. Effective diversification reduces extreme price fluctuations and smoothes out returns.

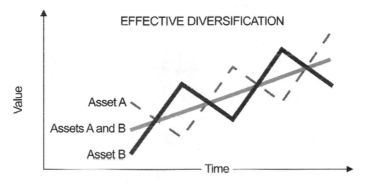

Figure 12-2. Effective diversification.

Imagine that Asset A in the figure above was your investment in farmland and that Asset B represented an investment in stocks. You might see the above effect. Over the long-term, owning a variety of different investments is the best strategy for the investor trying to achieve investment success.

PRINCIPLE 2:   ASSET ALLOCATION

Asset allocation simply means determining what proportion of your money is going to be invested in which asset classes—stocks, bonds, and cash investments—to maximize the growth of your portfolio. This may be the single most important determinant of the long-term performance of any investment portfolio. However, confusion occurs when the terms "asset allocation" and "diversification" are used interchangeably. Even if you are 100% invested in money market funds, it is still a form of asset allocation.

How do you determine what percentage of each asset class you should own? The largest determinant of performance is asset allocation or how money is divided among different asset categories.

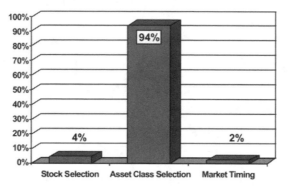

Figure 12-3. Illustration of asset allocation.

A study found that 94% of returns came from asset allocation. In 1986 Gary Hood and Gilbert Beebower analyzed the performance variations of 91 large pension funds. Their report analyzed the three primary investment strategies that determine variations in portfolio performance: market timing, security selection, and asset allocation. What the study discovered was that the two strategies that had the least impact on performance variation were market timing and security selection. Market timing and security selection activities rely on attempts to predict the future. Most of Wall Street's recommendations are based on these two strategies. Wall Street firms spend billions of dollars each year trying to outguess their competition in these two areas. To determine how much to put in each depends on your timeline, risk tolerance, and long-term rates of returns.

PRINCIPLE 3: TIMELINE

The longer the time period you hold your investments, the closer you will come to the expected average return. This means market fluctuations get smoothed out over time.

No serious investor knowingly holds a stock for only one day, one month, or even one year. Such brief time periods are clearly too short for stock investment. That is because the expected variation in returns is too large in comparison with the average expected return. Such short-term holdings in stocks are not investments. They are speculations.

Equities (stocks) become much less volatile the longer they are held. Bonds and money market funds have lower risk, lower returns, and can be held for a shorter period of time.

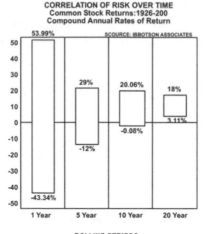

Figure 12-4. Correlation of risk over time.

If you study this chart, you will see that the common stock investments made in any one-year period could have gone up 54% or dropped 43%. However, when you look at any 20-year period, you can see that there are no down years—only gains.

If you measure an investment every three years, rather than every quarter, you can see satisfactory progress that would not be apparent in a quarterly measurement. In most cases, the timeline that investors use as the standard to measure results is far too short, causing dissatisfaction with investment performance.

PRINCIPLE 4: COMPOUNDING

Compounding is the process of earning a rate of return on your money that is invested and then reinvesting those earnings to realize an aggregate rate of return. This can be done with dividends, interest, or new contributions. For example, a $100 investment earning compound interest at 10% a year would total $110 at the end of the first year, and $121 at the end of the second year, and so on. The actual formula is:

compound sum = (principal) (1 + interest rate),
to the Nth power.
(Where N is the number of years)

The essence of the formula is that, on a regular basis, a return is earned not only on the original amount, but also on all previously accumulated earnings. You earn a return on your return. The typical compounding table below shows you how a single investment of $10,000 grows at various rates of return. You might get 5% from a bond, 10% from the stock market, and 16% over the last 20 years.

Table 12-3. Return on Your Investment with Compounding

Year	5%	10%	15%
1	$10,000	$10,000	$10,000
5	$12,800	$16,100	$20,100
10	$16,300	$25,900	$40,500
15	$20,800	$41,800	$81,400
20	$33,900	$108,300	$329,200

A simple way to figure how long it takes your money to double is the Rule of 72. Divide the number 72 by the interest rate, or rate of return, you anticipate earning. The result is the number of years it takes your money to double. For example, if you are earning 10%, your money will double in 7.2 years. If you are earning 12%, it takes only six years for your money to double.

Imagine a pond in your garden with a floating lily pad that doubles in size every day. If it takes 80 days for the lily to cover the pond entirely, on which day is half the pond still uncovered, open to the sun, and the outside? The answer is on the 79th day. The power of compounding is merely a function of time.

If you just look at accumulating money and do not factor in compounding, you are missing an important principle. Your goal is to maximize the rate of return for a given level of risk.

PRINCIPLE 5: REBALANCING

The principle of rebalancing is to maintain a proportionate percentage of the various asset classes that comprise your portfolio, maintaining proper diversification. By rebalancing, you may sacrifice some short-term gains by reducing your holdings of winning stocks prematurely, but you will also miss the big losses if they collapse. Although the mechanics of rebalancing are fairly straightforward, there are numerous methods that could be used to reach that optimal portfolio goal of maximizing returns while minimizing risk.

Many investment advisors rebalanced their equity positions down to their allocation targets as the bull market pushed equity values upward. Then, last year they increased equity positions as the declining markets dropped those positions below targets. As a result, they have been selling high, then buying low. When the price is down, you are able to buy more shares. Plus, you are reinvesting the money you have made along with your principal and compounding your growth.

Rebalancing an investment portfolio seems simple on the surface, but as you start to think through the method—frequency, tolerance limits, fees, and commissions—it becomes more complex. This is probably not an exercise that an average investor would pursue on his or her own. Here is where a qualified advisor can help. An investment advisor or consultant should be knowledgeable about the various issues surrounding rebalancing and, ideally, should be able to explain them to you in a way that makes the principle acceptable and practical.

SUMMARY

Diversification, asset allocation, timeline compounding, and rebalancing are principles that work together to level out the roller-coaster ride associated with up and down markets. They produce steady results, but you still need to understand your investment choices.

part 6
THE COMPREHENSIVE SUCCESSION SOLUTION

The Comprehensive Succession Solution is comprised of six parts designed to create multigenerational wealth. The parts are discovery, objective, blueprint, specific instructions, implementation, and the three R's. Each part is integral to your succession plan.

chapter **13**
COMPREHENSIVE SUCCESSION SOLUTION

Comprehensive succession planning covers every aspect of your financial life—from financial security to business planning, from retirement planning to estate planning, from investments to potential catastrophes. A succession plan serves as a solid foundation supporting the continuity of your family business.

DISCOVERY

Discovery is the most important step in the succession planning process. It is an inventory of your current situation. Discovery involves an accounting of any succession plans to date. It is a time to assess questions such as: Are you prepared for the succession of your farm? It is designed to generate thoughts, feelings, and hopes for succession. Before any action can be taken, you must know where you are both financially and emotionally. Where are you in relation to family concerns, business management, employee relationships, and financial resources? Discovery may involve questionnaires and worksheets to firm up attitudes, feelings, and ideas. Many people have completed some parts and pieces of a succession plan, but most families have not designed a comprehensive approach to succession planning. The planning tool below will help with your assessment.

Table 13-1. Discovery Planning Tool

Rank each in level of importance & priority...　　(1-low, 5-high)
Business Goals:
1. To ensure that the farm/agribusiness remains in the family.

　　　　　　　　　　　　　　　　　　　　　　　　　　　_____

2. To make the transition to new ownership/management transparent to our customers, clients, strategic alliances, and third party vendors.　　　　　　　　　　　　　　_____
3. To minimize the cost/associated expense of transition. _____
4. Other:　　　　　　　　　　　　　　　　　　　　　_____
　　Notes:

Ownership Succession:
1. To transfer ownership within _____ years.　　　　_____
2. To ensure that loyal employees are offered an opportunity for continued employment and/or the opportunity of an ownership interest.　　　　　　　　　　　　　　　　　　_____
3. If a partnership, to acquire other interest if/when available.

　　　　　　　　　　　　　　　　　　　　　　　　_____
4. To minimize income tax due to ownership transition.

　　　　　　　　　　　　　　　　　　　　　　　　_____
5. To receive fair market value for ownership interest if sold.

　　　　　　　　　　　　　　　　　　　　　　　　_____
6. To continue receiving an income following transition.

　　　　　　　　　　　　　　　　　　　　　　　　_____
7. To reduce exposure to business liabilities.　　　_____
8. Avoid gift tax, minimize estate tax and transfer obligations.

　　　　　　　　　　　　　　　　　　　　　　　　_____
9. Other:　　　　　　　　　　　　　　　　　　　_____
　　Notes:

Management Succession:
1. To transition to new management in _____ years.　_____
2. To transition management control to _____

　　　　　　　　　　　　　　　　　　　　　　　　_____
3. In case of premature death or disability _____ should continue to run the operation until _____ is ready to assume the role.
4. Other:　　　　　　　　　　　　　　　　　　　_____
Notes:

Wealth Accumulation:
1. To develop an investment program. _____
2. To protect assets through contingency planning. _____
3. To provide a college education for children/grandchildren.

_____
4. Leave a meaningful legacy to _____ organization.

_____
5. Other: _____
   Notes:

Retirement or the next venture in your vocational life:
1. To accumulate an investment portfolio that I cannot outgrow.

_____
2. To retire by/on _____. _____
3. To move on to the next venture in my vocational life by _____.

_____
4. To provide an income of $_____ adjusted for inflation.

_____
5. Other: _____
Notes:

Estate Planning:
1. To efficiently pass the assets of my estate. _____
2. To minimize estate tax and transfer obligations. _____
3. To contribute to _____ charitable bequest. _____
4. To provide for the special needs of _____. _____
5. Other: _____
   Notes:

The discovery process begins with a complete outline of the succession planning process. The Comprehensive Succession Solutions is a cycle that is revised and refined with the dynamics of family and business. It is designed to flex as needed to suit the dynamics of a growing family and an increasingly complex business environment.

The process begins with the discovery phase, followed closely by a detail of your objectives. From your objectives, a blueprint is designed to help map your strategies. With the blueprint, a list of instructions (actionable steps) can be developed. Finally, you should establish a consistent review schedule.

Case Study (Part 1)

Andy Carlisle, 66, is the sole shareholder of Carlisle Farms, Inc., a vertically integrated cotton producer. Due to the development of a proprietary wholesaling system, Carlisle Farms, Inc., has been able to sustain annual growth rates that exceed the industry norm. Andy is married and has two children. Mary, his wife of 42 years, is a homemaker, and she volunteers at the local elementary school. Nicole, 30, his daughter, is an accountant. She has worked for Carlisle Farms for the past 5 years. Nicole would eventually like to run the business. Michael, his son, a local medical doctor, has no interest in an ownership role in the business.

Andy is in good health. He enjoys the challenges and rewards of the business and intends to remain active in the business into the foreseeable future. His business goal is to transfer ownership to his daughter Nicole. His estate planning goal is to provide financially for his wife, if he predeceases her. Any remaining wealth would be divided between their children, Nicole and Michael.

Andy and Mary's Assets

Assets	Andy	Mary
Carlisle Farms Incorporated	$6,000,000	
Home (tenants in common)	225,000	$225,000
Cash (tenants in common)	112,000	112,000
Mutual funds (tenants in common)	210,000	210,000
Life insurance cash value	92,000	127,000
Total	$6,639,000	$674,000

A multidisciplinary team of professionals can guide you through the process. As no single professional can provide all of the detail necessary to design and implement a Com-prehensive Succession Solution, one professional serves as "conductor" leading the team of professionals. The conductor coordinates the implementation of your succession plan.

The process begins with an overview involving you, your advisor, and multiple generations of your family. A Comprehensive Succession Solution must include multiple generations of your family to be considered complete. Each decision affects your entire family. The decisions you make today will affect your family for generations to come.

OBJECTIVE

Every action is preceded by a decision to act "by design or default." Some people refer to this concept as proactive verses reactive management. You can act to avert crises or you can react to the demands of a given situation.

Unfortunately, many people live by default. They are constantly predicating their actions on the crisis of the moment. In business I refer to this as crisis management. As a successful businessperson you must avoid crises management. You are most successful when your purpose is focused and you know exactly what outcome you want to achieve.

Detailing your objectives is a form of sharing your vision. It is through sharing that we find inspiration. If inspiration is the apotheosis of your vision, vision becomes the foundation of your plan. In sharing your vision, you clarify the critical points of your plan. Enlisting others to share in your vision allows you to develop the synergy necessary to complete the planning process. Comprehensive succession planning is always a collaborative effort. You must involve multiple generations, a variety of professionals, and your loyal employees.

Spelling out your objectives forces you to consider every aspect of your vision. Details become the focus of action. The process of writing your objectives forces you to become aware of your hopes and dreams. Many of us carry inspiring aspirations. Instead of reaching for our aspirations, we settle for less. Explore what you want to accomplish, set the goal, build a plan, and then finish it.

You explore your objectives as they relate to personal growth, business development, management succession, estate planning, and contingency planning. Comprehensive succession planning involves personal and family issues relative to your business.

Committing your objectives to paper begins the process of collecting hard data. This step focuses on collecting the facts of your situation, including money, savings, retirement plans, fixed and variable business expenses, gross/net income, investments, outstanding loans, accounts payable/receivable, insurance plans, and an assessment of your investment risk tolerance. When you share specific information, you touch both your immediate family and the various generations through your succession plan. Employees are also included in this phase of the planning.

Table 13-2. Your Assets

Category	Asset	His ($)	Hers ($)	Titled	Objective ($)
Business	Fair market value				
	Real estate				
	Business property				
	Inventory				
	Accounts receivable				
Personal assets	Primary residence				
	Secondary residence				
	Personal property				
	Vehicles/ boats/toys				
	Jewelry				
Cash equivalents	Checking and savings Accounts				
	Money market instruments				

	Mutual funds/ETF/ stocks				
	Other liquid assets				
Retirement assets	IRAs/Roth IRAs				
	Retirement plans-vested				
	401(k) plans				
	Stock Options/ purchase Plans				
	Tax-deferred annuities				
Other investments	Rental residential and commercial				
	Undeveloped land				
	Other				
Life insurance	Cash value life Insurance				
Any other business assets					
Total					

Note.—H, husband; W, wife; JT, joint tenancy; JTWROS, joint tenants with right of survivorship; CP, community property; T, irrevocable trust; TC, tenants in common.

A review of any prior planning will be addressed in this step. We have all done some form of prior planning.

The parts and pieces of prior planning efforts may be a beginning point for building a comprehensive plan.

Comprehensive Plan Checklist
Copies may be requested of the following:
Tax returns, the last 3 years _____
Wills/trusts/legal instruments _____
Financial statements _____
Life/disability/health/LTCI policies _____
Power of attorney/appointment _____
Guardian nominations _____
Separation/divorce/nuptial agreements _____
Retirement plan information/statements _____
Brokerage/mutual fund statements _____
Appraisals _____

A complete plan will consider all "interested" parties in the process. Interested persons are your sons, daughters, brothers, sisters, parents, and grandparents (i.e., multiple generations of your extended family). Interested persons also include key employees, some business alliances, third-party vendors, or the bank. If succession involves a sale or transition to an outside interest, potential suitors may be included in this phase.

Table 13-3. Family: Children, Grandchildren, Parents, and In-Laws

Name	Address	Marital Status	Relation- ship	Employment

Table 13-4. Loyal Employees

Name	Address	Tenure	Position

This step is about gathering information and clarifying your objectives. No advice is given. It is designed first to define the vision that you have for transitioning your business to the next generation. The focus is on learning what is important to you.

- What do you want your legacy to look like?
- Who do you want involved in the process and how do you "maximize your legacy?"
- What do you want to achieve through a Comprehensive Succession Solution?

Table 13-5. Objectives

(#)	Objectives Clearly Defined	Achievement Date
1		
2		
3		
4		
5		
6		
7		

BLUEPRINT

As the architect designs a building, a succession planner designs a succession solution. To initiate the process, you are given checklists similar to the one below. It is the job of a financial planner to work with you to assemble the data. Patience is required, especially when affairs are complex. "Scattered assets" are the farmer's norm and at times it may take more time to gather data than to complete the plan. However, a thorough process of gathering information pays big dividends.

Case Study (Part 2)

After cursory discussions regarding Andy's goals, he decided that his comprehensive succession plan must achieve the following objectives:

1. Ensure that Mary continues to receive an income, comparable to their current income, in the event Andy predeceases her.
2. Gradually transfer ownership of Carlisle Farms, Inc., to Nicole.
3. Provide the necessary funds so Nicole may purchase the business.
4. Be sure Nicole develops the skills and abilities necessary to expand the business successfully.
5. Provide for an equitable distribution of wealth to Michael.
6. Minimize the estate taxes and transfer obligations. Ensure that liquid capital is available to pay all taxes.
7. Plan for the contingencies of premature death or disability, including long-term care.

Gathering basic data encompasses but should not be limited to the following:

1. *Family census.* Names, residence and farm addresses, contact information (phone, fax, e-mail), names of children, ages and dates of birth for all family members, and Social Security numbers. Are children married? Grandchildren? Health status? Special needs?

2. *Net worth statement.* Determine ownership for all assets (i.e., ownership by client, spouse, or partner), joint ownership (define such as JTWROS, TIC, community property), trusts (define), and other (define, such as accounts held for minors). Copies may be requested of all statements.

3. Checking, savings, money market, and CDs.

4. *Farm real estate.* Include residence, additional properties. Identify owner, purchase price, current value, mortgage terms, current balance, and cash flow from farm properties.

5. *Farm partnerships.* Obtain copy of recent quarterly or annual report. Determine cash flow, tax benefits, estimated values, and liquidity, if any.

6. *Other farm related business interests.* Name, type of business, form of ownership (C-corp., S-corp., sole proprietor, partnership, LLC), percentage of ownership, value of interest, buy/sell agreement, or succession plan?

7. *Personal assets.* Description (tractors, trucks, car, aircraft), value, and debt. Values of other assets such as jewelry and household furnishings may be requested.

8. *Retirement plans.* Obtain statements for all pension/profit sharing plans, IRAs; 401(k), or deferred compensation plans. Specify primary and contingent beneficiaries.

9. *Stocks, bonds, and mutual funds* (list or provide brokerage or custodial statement). Include data on U.S. Savings Bonds. Obtain tax basis for all securities.

10. *Annuities* (fixed and variable). Obtain copy of policy and recent quarterly and annual reports. Determine owner, annuitant, primary and contingent beneficiaries, and tax status.

11. *Life insurance.* Request copy of policy, original proposal, last annual report. Determine type of policy, face amount, the insured, owner, beneficiary (primary and contingent), premium payments, adequacy of payments (how long will the policy carry given current assumptions?), purpose of the coverage, cash values if applicable (current value, surrender value, loans outstanding). Include data on group insurance and any coverage tied to employer benefits or business arrangements such as buy/sell agreements. Determine all sources of death benefits.

12. *Education planning.* Section 529 Plans, Education IRAs, and other.

13. *Tangibles.* Type of asset (precious metals, gems, coins), date of purchase, original investment, and current value.

14. *Other insurance.* Include copies of homeowner, rental, auto, umbrella liability policies; personal and group disability policies, and long-term care.

15. *Copies of legal documents and other key documents.* Wills, trusts (including revocable or irrevocable living trusts, charitable trusts), durable powers of attorney for assets and health care, divorce decrees, alimony and child support agreements, prenuptial agreements, purchase agreements, farm buy/sell agreements, family farming partnerships, and most recent tax return.

16. *Farmer's advisory team.* The name, address, and contact information for other key advisors such as a CPA or other tax adviser, attorney, banker, trustees, insurance agents, and brokers.

17. *Anything else you may feel is important* to you or anyone included in your family or among your loyal employees.

The comprehensive solution works through a multidisciplinary team of professionals. It is critical that the professionals work together. Coordination of efforts determines the outcome. Designing a plan that considers the advice brought by each professional is key.

The final result is a blueprint of your comprehensive business succession plan. Your final endorsement of the blueprint puts everything in motion. Once you see your goals on paper, you are on the way to maximizing your legacy.

SPECIFIC INSTRUCTIONS

Action is the key to success! Your plan should detail specific actionable steps. Each step must be coordinated with the others for a complete transition. Each recommmendation should be designed to address your goals.

Table 13-6. Sample Action Plan			
Goal:_____			
Steps	Action	Who	Completion Date

IMPLEMENTATION

Action on paper elevates the level of commitment to the succession process. Seeing the steps you will take to implement your plan may feel a bit overwhelming. Most of the effort so far has been talk. Now you are taking action and implementing what may be difficult decisions.

Table 13-7. Action Progress Sheet

Step	Specific Action Plan	Completion Date	Checked By
	(Specific action plan)		
	(Specific action plan)		
	(Specific action plan)		
	(Specific action plan)		
	(Specific action plan)		

This step may seem a bit academic, yet it is important. Implementation is the moment of truth in the transition plan. Applying the details of a plan that will affect the future of your business and the lives of your heirs is a vital responsibility. Attention to detail is imperative. Like subcontractors on a large construction project, each member of your succession team must meet their respective deadlines. One factor may be dependent on the next. The professional orchestrating your transition plan must insure a smooth and timely transition.

Case Study (Part 3)

Providing income for Mary in the event Andy predeceases her is the objective tackled here. Providing income for a surviving spouse is often the first estate planning goal for married couples. However, when the household income and a significant portion of the couple's wealth are derived from a business, providing income to a nonworking surviving spouse can be challenging.

Andy knows that Mary may not be comfortable depending on the business for financial support when she has neither the desire nor the ability to run it. Family dynamics are dicey. Mary and Nicole have a tense relationship. Expecting Nicole to run the business profitably while her mother receives an income will inevitably lead to conflict. Mary may tend to second-guess Nicole's business decisions. Nicole may become resentful that the business is supporting Mary when she does not contribute to it. Andy wants to be sure Nicole can buy the business upon his death. The proceeds from the sale would then be invested to generate a consistent income for Mary.

The responsibility of the conductor orchestrating your succession plan evolves from initiation and design to that of coordinator of implementation. He or she will oversee the implementation steps and confirm completion by each member of your team.

REVIEW, REVISE, AND REFINE

Everything changes:
- Your business will change
- Your family will change
- Tax laws change

The investment of thought, time, and money will only be valuable if your plans operate according to your objectives. The conductor of your professional advisory team should meet with you no less than annually to review, revise, and refine your business succession plan. Annual reviews allow for changes that may occur within your business, your family, or tax law.

LEGACY BY D

chapter **14**
YOUR PLANNING TEAM

Comprehensive succession planning is a very complex field. The various dimensions required to draft then implement a comprehensive succession plan are as varied as there are people involved in farming. In fact, the family dimension of a family agribusiness causes issues relating to money, ownership, and management to be emotionally charged.

THE PLANNING TEAM

Comprehensive succession planning includes business planning, financial planning, estate planning, ownership/management succession, and retirement planning. The science that supports succession planning is a clear understanding of money, tax law, and estate planning technique. The art that ties the plan together, like baling wire around straw, is comprised of communication, planning, people, and intuition. It may be very difficult to find one person who is capable of providing both the multidisciplinary science and the interpersonal art necessary to complete your comprehensive succession plan. You need to build a team of professionals, licensed and trained experts, to assist your succession planning efforts. Your team may include a financial planner, estate planning attorney, certified public accountant, trust officer, and banker. Your team may include any number of confidential professional advisors that you deem necessary.

FINANCIAL PLANNER

Any number of financial advisors may use the title financial planner. The persons referred to here are certified financial planners (CFP®s) or a certified public accountants (CPAs) who has earned the personal financial planner (PFP) designation. CFP®s/CPA-PFPs are educated in financial planning, including academic education in money, investments, estate planning, retirement, taxes, education, and business planning. They are usually well versed in applying their academic training to assisting people with planning situations (such as business succession planning).

ESTATE PLANNING ATTORNEY

Most attorneys can draft a basic will and any other legal document, but for comprehensive succession planning, you may want to consider an attorney who has special training and certification as an estate planning specialist. Tax laws and estate planning rules are in constant flux. Though a comprehensive succession plan is reviewed and revised on an annual basis, many of the factors inherent in the plan are designed for unforeseen contingencies. In the case of premature death, disability, or some cause that necessitates sudden action, you want a plan that is correctly designed.

CERTIFIED PUBLIC ACCOUNTANT (CPA)

As a successful businessperson, you are most likely currently associated with a CPA. A CPA who is well versed in your financial affairs is important for your business. As with any other job on the farm, the right tool makes a significant difference in the time and efficiency with which a task is completed. A CPA well versed in the intricacies of comprehensive succession planning will augment the planning and implementation process.

TRUST OFFICER

Many estate planning and business asset transition plans involve the use of a multiple legal trust. Each trust must designate a trustee, that is, a person to manage the assets of the trust. If you plan to use a corporate trustee, you may include a trust officer in the planning stages of your succession planning process. The experience and education of the trust officer may add an important dimension to your succession plan.

BANKER

As a successful businessperson, you may have a personal relationship with a banker, a person who has helped you make wise decisions regarding leveraged financing, production credit, and financial development. Including a banker with whom you have a personal relationship may help to clarify financial concepts and business capital needs. This person is often brought into the planning process to augment your personal viewpoints based on shared business history.

INSURANCE PROFESSIONAL

Much of a comprehensive succession plan is designed to compensate for disastrous contingencies. One person who can help you avert a financial disaster may be an insurance person. Whether it be premature death, disability, or a liability, an insurance professional is usually well versed in succession issues and may be in a position to offer protection.

Case Study (Part 4)

Upon his death, Andy wants Nicole to purchase any Carlisle Farms stock which remains in his investment portfolio. He has considered a corporate stock redemption at his death (gifting an interest to Nicole now to make her a stockholder so that upon redemption she owns 100% of Carlisle Farms, Inc.). Life insurance will play a significant role in funding the transfer of ownership to Nicole. Andy does not want the insurance proceeds to be paid directly to the corporation, subjecting the proceeds to the claims of creditors. As a corporation, Carlisle Farms, Inc., may be subject to alternative minimum tax if it owns the life insurance. After considering the alternatives, Andy has decided that Nicole should purchase the stock rather than use a corporate redemption.

To establish a legitimate selling price and to ensure that Nicole is legally bound to purchase the stock, Andy and Nicole enter into a buy/sell agreement. Because of their relationship, Andy and Nicole are careful in structuring the agreement so that the sales price is recognized by the Internal Revenue Service (IRS). Recall that if the IRS determines that the stock's true estate tax value is higher than the value established in the buy/sell agreement, the estate may be taxed at the higher value. To avoid this unfavorable consequence, the buy/sell agreement stipulates that the stock will be purchased at fair market value (FMV) upon death. The FMV will be determined by a professional business appraiser.

Note: Designating the business buyout at FMV in the buy/sell agreement reduces the risk that the IRS will challenge the business valuation for estate tax purposes. A buyout based on a FMV established by a professional business appraiser also relieves some of the tension between the surviving spouse and other members of the family. The disadvantage to stipulating a purchase at FMV (a moving target) instead of a fixed value is determining the amount of life insurance needed to fund the buyout.

The agreement further stipulates that Nicole will make a down payment equal to the lesser of the life insurance proceeds or FMV at the time of death. Any outstanding balance will be paid to the estate, or the beneficiary of the estate, over 10 years and subject to the current lending rate used by XYZ bank.

Andy and Mary immediately begin an annual gifting program to transfer stock to Nicole on a regular basis. They are allowed, through gift-splitting, to transfer (gift) up to $22,000, or $11,000 each, in stock each year. The process of regular gifting offers two advantages. First, Andy decreases his estate tax and transfer obligations in the event of his death. He removes $22,000 worth of appreciating asset from his estate each year. Probate expenses—often based on estate value—are also reduced. Andy maintains the controlling interest in Carlisle Farms, Inc. Secondly, Andy knows that Nicole as a share-holder (partial owner) will take more interest in the growth and development of the business.

SELECTING A PLANNER

Aside from the professions discussed above, one person must be selected by you to conduct and orchestrate the various professionals who comprise your succession planning team. That person must be well versed in a cross-disciplinary approach to planning, must be able to tap the energy of several professionals to serve your end objective, must become counsel to multiple generations of your immediate and extended family, and must have your confidence and trust.

A well-designed business succession plan may be the most important thing you do to guarantee that your legacy is passed to the heirs of your choice under the circumstances of your choosing. The planner who coordinates the planning process will act as coach, confidant, and expert to multiple generations of your family. The most important decision you make, following the decision to implement the planning process, is who should act in that capacity. Does that person have the right credentials, experience, and education to support your objectives and the duties of the role?

So you have decided that a business succession plan is a good idea. You know that planning now for tomorrow's ownership increases the value and long-term viability of your farm business. Implementing a business succession plan allows you to groom your successor. It assures continuity of the business. Planning allows the opportunity to pass the farm to the heirs of your choice under circumstances chosen by you. Correct planning ensures that your successors are not forced to drain important capital, sell valuable assets, or secure onerous loans to settle the estate taxes and transfer obligations.

To take action is the most important decision you can make in the planning process. Finding the right planner to orchestrate the facets of the succession planning process is a challenge. Most people spend more time shopping for a new pair of boots than they do shopping for a professional advisor! Boots are infinitely easier to find and far less expensive, yet you can spend hours driving from one store to the next in search of the perfect pair. While the right boots may seem important, there is no comparison to the magnitude of your succession plan.

How do most people find an advisor? The most popular way is by way of a friend or a neighbor who has a planner, accountant, or attorney helping them with a succession plan. You trust this neighbor. He has made good decisions in the past, so you follow his recommendation and contact the planner who is working with his family.

The second way people find an advisor is through the yellow pages. They call someone completely out of the blue, usually based on the layout of an advertisement in the phone book. This should be followed up with a thorough interview to decide whether this person is right for your situation. Compatibility between your family and your succession planning advisor is important.

Before making the decision about who should act as your planner, you should define what you expect him to do. You can expect a planner to do the research and due diligence. Comprehensive succession planning covers money, taxes, estate, retirement, and financial planning. The homework required to address some of the details of succession planning is at times overwhelming to the uninitiated. A good planner leads that charge, ensuring that options are not overlooked and no details are ignored.

Key Point: Role of an Effective Planner

- Assemble a multidisciplinary team of professionals to include, but not limited to, financial planner, accountant, attorney, and others as the situation demands.

- Lead discussions, interviews and meetings with owners, management, other professionals, and family.

- Delegate responsibilities to others and assure that planning is completed in a timely manner.

- Coordinate a multidisciplinary team and other professionals ensuring an efficient and effective succession planning outcome.
- Coordinate the succession planning process, including implementation and communication.

- Facilitate regular follow-up. Review and, if necessary, revise the plan in accordance with current tax law, business environment, and family dynamics.
- Stay abreast of latest developments in planning techniques, tax laws, and business law to adjust plans as necessary.

Case Study (Part 5)

Though Nicole will be purchasing Carlisle Farms, Inc., she does not have enough cash to purchase the stock outright. An installment sale will not solve Mary and Nicole's problems. Andy plans to purchase life insurance and name Nicole as the beneficiary. To keep the proceeds from Andy's estate, he establishes an irrevocable life insurance trust to own the life insurance policy. Since Andy is gifting his full annual exclusion amount in stock to Nicole, the premium payment will reduce his lifetime exclusion amount of $1,500,000

Andy decides that, although the business is currently valued at $6 million, a $5 million life insurance adequately covers the buyout obligation. The $5 million insurance proceeds, combined with other assets, provide a comfortable income for Mary and a cushion to offset future inflation. The premium for the policy will not break the bank. Although no one likes to pay an insurance premium, the cost to fund this policy is within reason considering the benefit it provides in the over all succession solution. The business is currently growing. The proceeds do not exceed the value of the business. Finally, if more money is needed to complete the purchase, Nicole will borrow from other sources, considering the ratio of capital to borrowed money.

Use the following checklist as an interview guide for selecting an advisor. The purpose of this questionnaire is to initiate a discussion between you and the planner candidates. First, discussion results will help you to decide whether you can trust this person. Second, can this person develop a comprehensive business succession plan? Finally, are there any discrepancies in this persons resume?

CHECKLIST

1. Do you have experience providing advice on business succession planning including:
   - ☐ Business planning
   - ☐ Retirement planning
   - ☐ Estate planning
   - ☐ Investment planning
   - ☐ Insurance planning

Notes:_____

_____

_____

Though we tend to assume that time/tenure is an important measure of experience, I usually advise people to look for experience. Does the person you are considering have the breadth and depth of experience to manage the circumstances of your succession situation successfully? Is this person versed in the academic areas, including business, retirement, estate, investment, and insurance planning?

2. What qualifies you to act as a specialist in the field of business succession planning?

Notes:_____

_____

_____

Using the title "financial planner," "advisor," or "counselor" does not make a person qualified to handle your situation. You must look for a person who has the education, skill, and experience to bring your succession plan to fruition, abiding by your conditions. Formal education to support a person's professional vocation is key. Academic knowledge is important to support the recommendations made. A CFP® (Certified Financial Planner®) is educated to assist with the various aspects of financial planning. A CPA PFP (Certified Public Accountant

Personal Financial Planner) is similarly educated. Experience with business, retirement, estate, investment, and insurance planning is important. A revealing question to ask each prospective planner is: What do you do to stay current? Meeting the minimum state/federal license continuing education requirements is not enough to meet the demands of the dynamic financial services marketplace.

3. How long have you been offering business succession planning advice?
   □ Less than one year
   □ One to four years
   □ Five to ten years
   □ More than 10 years

Notes:_____

_____

_____

Time is important as a measure of experience. Comprehensive succession planning is incredibly broad and highly specialized. Time as an oversimplified measure of experience may point to a level of competency.

4. For how many families do you currently provide business succession planning?
   □ Less than 10
   □ 10 to 39
   □ 40 to 79
   □ 80 +

Notes:_____

_____

_____

There are two reasons this question may be important. The most obvious is a question of experience. Do you help enough successful farm/agribusiness families so that your situation is not an experiment? Secondly, do you help so many families that I will not get the time and attention my situation may deserve?

5. Give me a brief overview of your career in financial services.

Notes:_____

_____

_____

Most planners have a Curriculum Vitae available to prospective clients. Review and then ask appropriate clarification questions. You are hiring a family coach, confidant, and counselor—someone who will sort through the biggest issues you face in planning your business transition.

6. What are your educational qualifications? Briefly describe areas of study/specialization.

Notes:_____

_____

_____

Education is the foundation for technical expertise. A planner must become educated in succession planning and then he must remain current as laws change. A planner must be diligent in the quest for more information in order to serve a clientele effectively.

7. What financial planning designations or certificates do you hold?
☐ Certified Financial Planner® (CFP®)
☐ Certified Public Accountant–Personal Financial

☐ Planner (CPA-PFP)
☐ Chartered Financial Consultant (ChFC)
☐ Other_____

Notes:_____
_____

How far has this person gone to become a recognized professional in financial planning?

8. Other than required continuing education hours, how many hours do you study regularly in your field of professional expertise?

Notes:_____
_____

Case Study (Part 6)

Nicole obviously has the academic education to support her role at Carlisle. She has worked with the company for five years (probably more considering high school jobs and part-time employment). She definitely has the desire to succeed. She needs some formal coaching, mentoring, and even classroom training to assume the helm as leader. Andy assesses Nicole's strengths, her leadership competencies, and her abilities as a Chief Executive Officer (CEO), using a leadership skills inventory. He devises a plan to prepare Nicole for the role she will gradually assume as owner/manager (President) of Carlisle Farms, Inc.

Owner/Manager Development Plan

Skill/Ability	Specific Action	Who	Date	Level 1-5
Communications	Attend community college Writing for Business workshop	Instructor	09/15-09/18	
Farm safety	Attend Farm Safety Workshop sponsored by John Deere	Instructor	02/01-02/03	
Business planning/ vision	Work with current owners/ department managers through the planning process for the coming year	Tom & Steve	10/01-01/31	
People skills/ teamwork	Assume responsibility for harvest crew. Work closely with Alfredo and the other team managers	Alfredo and others	07/15-09/30	
Crop rotation	Assist in plan for next years' crop cycle	Tom & Steve	10/01-11/30	
Water management	Attend water board meeting with Tom; assess coming years concerns and plan accordingly	Water Board and Tom	Monthly	

> Nicole also will be asked to attend all meetings regarding employee relations, banking, business planning, and customer/client interaction. She must become familiar with the administration of the farming and business operation.
>
> For his part, Andy realizes that he cannot provide much of the training that Nicole will need. So, in the interest of better training and improved management team development, he establishes a mentoring relationship with some of the other management personnel at Carlisle.

9. What licenses do you hold?
    - ☐ Insurance
    - ☐ Securities
    - ☐ CPA
    - ☐ J.D. (Juris Doctorate: Attorney)
    - ☐ Other_____

Notes:_____
_____

Licensing dictates a breadth of available services. If a practitioner is licensed in several areas, he or she may see several alternatives to solve a problem or address a concern. If the only tool you have is a hammer, every problem you confront becomes a nail. A person licensed in multiple disciplines not only has a broad base of knowledge but also may have an understanding of how to tie together various pieces of a solution.

10. What services do you offer?

Notes:_____
_____
_____

SUCCESSION PLANNING FOR AGRIBUSINESS OWNERS

Services vary from person to person and firm to firm; you need an understanding of the limitations of the firm that you trust to address your succession planning. Is he or she positioned to handle each and every area required for your particular situation?

11. Briefly describe your approach to business succession planning.

Notes:_____

_____

_____

A good planner has a systematic way of approaching a succession situation. This question asks the planner to describe his approach.

12. Who will work directly with me?
□ Planner
□ Associate

Notes:_____

_____

_____

It is likely that some of your work will be handled by an associate. It is fair for you to know in what circumstances or under what conditions you may be working with an associate. It is also wise to inquire about the credentials and qualifications of associates. Having an additional set of eyes and ears examining your situation can be advantageous. Your primary planner must strike that fine balance between synergy—that creative energy generated when multiple people work on a problem using their various backgrounds and experiences—and "too many cooks spoil the broth." The latter is a committee-like solution to a simple problem.

13. Who will review my financial situation?
☐ Planner
☐ Associate
☐ Planning department personnel
☐ In-house accountants
☐ In-house attorney

Notes:_____

_____

_____

The previous section addressed the team approach necessary to address succession concerns on a comprehensive level. This question is designed to address the internal team supporting the planner. I refer to this as the infrastructure supporting his or her planning and investment products and services. You may ask, "Who else will be privy to my situation, and how will their input help?"

14. How do you get paid for services? Do you fully disclose your compensation schedule?
☐ Fee
☐ Commission
☐ Salary
☐ Other

Notes:_____

_____

_____

Full disclosure is a must in the financial services industry today. You should know not only how much a planner is being paid but also how fees are calculated. Many financial transactions are commodities. Simple trades and product transactions can be made by phone or computer. Advice and the proper use of various financial products are client specific. As an educated consumer, your job is to know what you are getting and how much it costs.

15. Do you have strategic alliances with other professionals to whom you may refer me? And do you receive a bonus or fee for the referral?
    ☐ Yes
    ☐ No

If yes, do you fully disclose this relationship and the bonus or fee?
    ☐ Yes
    ☐ No

Notes:_____

_____

_____

Comprehensive succession planning is a team effort. If you are referred to another professional to assist in the planning process, does the planner receive some form of referral fee or other form of remuneration? If so, the relationship and the payment should be disclosed.

16. Do you provide a written client engagement agreement?
    ☐ Yes
    ☐ No
Notes:_____

_____

_____

Most planners offer a client engagement letter. The letter serves as the foundation to a relationship between planner and client. A long-term client/planner relationship is critical to fulfilling the objectives of your succession plan. The letter designed to establish the basic parameters of that relationship is expected by both the client and the planner. It becomes the building block on which your succession plan is established.

SIX STEPS FOR A SUCCESSFUL TRANSITION

Congratulations - you've made it. You are well on your way to addressing the concerns every business owner must face. You are about to pass stewardship to the next generation. A successful transition may be the greatest reward you realize in your working career. The depth of your conviction will be measured by the motivating power of your desire. The following seven steps will help you meet each challenge head on.

Case Study (Part 7)

Michael has no interest in participating in the business of Carlisle Farms, Inc. He is a successful medical doctor running his own practice. Andy and Mary tell Michael of their intention to transition the business to Nicole, including a management role and an ownership interest. They explain that though she will receive some immediate financial consideration (gifts), he will not receive an inheritance until both parents pass away, and the estate is settled. Michael understands that Nicole will receive an inheritance, but also that she is committed to Carlisle Farms, Inc. She will dedicate time and energy to the farming operation to grow the business into the future. She may forgo a potentially higher income in order to do this. This is a form of deferred business equity.

Andy and Mary decide that Michael should receive the first $5,000,000 from the estate of the second to die. That amount is equal to the amount of life insurance Nicole received to purchase the business. Any residual estate assets should be divided equally between the two children.

STEP 1: TAKE ACTION

Have you determined exactly what you want? Then pledge to make it happen. Define a shared vision with your family, and seek a common dedication to that vision. Without a firm commitment, anything can happen. By committing to a goal, you focus all of your resources to make sure you achieve the results you want.

Most family businesses decisions, changes, and improvements are made as knee-jerk reactions. The culture you create dictates the attitude in which all aspects of your business life are viewed. With every action you take, ask yourself if it is consistent with what you want to achieve, the culture you want to create, and the values you want to see perpetuated.

STEP 2: FORM A COMMITTED COALITION WITHIN YOUR FAMILY

Form a coalition of all family members and contact all interested or involved heirs. It is not only your eldest son who may be your senior management prospect, but potentially everyone who is involved directly or indirectly in the family business.

Do not underestimate the time and attention you need to form a dedicated coalition. Remember when you begin creating your coalition you have had a lot of time to clarify your vision and the direction you plan to move the farm operation. Each of your interested heirs will hear your vision for the first time. You need to allow them the time to reach their own conclusions and to help them make your commitment a reality.

STEP 3: CLEARLY ENVISION YOUR LEGACY

Paint a picture of what your life is going to look like when your journey is complete. What picture symbolizes the legacy you will leave? Many employees and relatives who are part of your farm team today may have difficulty understanding the what, who, and how of the changes your farm business is about to undergo. They will be keenly interested in how is this transition going to affect them?

How do you see your future? Your imagination allows you to visualize what you would like your farm/agribusiness to look like five years from now. The ability to visualize the result you are seeking help to reinforce the commitment that you will make to design your succession plan. It also helps your interested heirs to assist you in building your shared vision of the future.

STEP 4: BEGIN THE TRANSITION

If you have decided that you want to design and then implement a comprehensive succession plan this year, what action will it take to begin the process? Consult with a professional who specializes in succession planning or hold a family meeting to discuss your intention. As a result of the family meeting, you may assign various tasks to family members to research more specifically the ramifications of comprehensive succession planning. For many, this commitment might seem overwhelming, due to all that must be accomplished. However, a succession plan can become a reality merely by dividing it into manageable steps.

Case Study (Part 8)

Recall that Andy has no intention of relinquishing control of the corporation during his lifetime. As a major asset, the source of all of their income and financial support, the business is vital to Andy and Mary. The stock that Andy retains, his controlling interest, will not be discounted due to a minority interest, so his estate tax obligation reflects the full value of his ownership shares in the business.

Andy designs a basic estate plan. He uses a will to establish testamentary (at death) A-B trusts. The trusts—working in conjunction with the irre-vocable life insurance trust (ILIT) and the buy/sell agreement—efficiently pass the business to Nicole. Upon Andy's death, Nicole receives $5,000,000 in life insurance proceeds to buy the business from Mary (the estate). A $1,500,000 (applicable exclusion amount) goes into the Credit Shelter Trust, thereby sheltering it from estate taxes. The balance passes to Mary in the marital trust. Andy and Mary are comfortable that the estate of the second to die will have sufficient cash to pay any estate tax or transfer obligation.

Recall that Michael will not receive any assets until the second death. Then he will receive an amount equal to

---

the life insurance that Nicole received at Andy's death plus one half of the balance of the estate.

At some point in the future, a revision may necessitate the establishment of a Grantor Retained Annuity Trust (GRAT) or an IDIT once Andy is willing to relinquish some control. Successful change is a real challenge because no one reacts well to change except maybe the person who is initiating it.

STEP 5: ACCELERATE THE PACE

Create a sense of urgency. Once you have made the decision to implement a comprehensive succession plan, or any other decision to improve, it is your job as leader is to move ahead. Let your family know that it is okay to feel uncomfortable and resistant to change, but the winners in business will always be the ones who most effectively adapt to the ebbs and flows of a changing environment.

STEP 6: COMMIT YOUR PLAN TO WRITING

Commit your plan to writing and end each meeting by answering the question. What's next?

SUMMARY

Your succession plan addresses changing the leadership of your business. How it will affect you fiscally, as well as your financial security, retirement plan, investment objectives, and your entire financial future are completely dependent on this decision. Your personal values and aspirations are realized through the strength of the choices you make now. The years of invested discipline, hard work, and dedication are demonstrated through this decision. Nothing is more critical to the future success of your business than the leader you select.

A strong management successor allows you more freedom in the business. A business with a management succession plan can command a premium price beyond that of a business without a plan. The transfer of intellectual property and cultural memory can only be made on purpose with a plan over time. A strong management successor protects that financial interest.

Case Study (Part 9)

Using the estate plan, Andy has established a contingency plan for premature death. The ILIT gives Nicole a sufficient amount of money to buy the business from Andy's estate. It also provides Mary with the income and financial support she needs. Disability presents another challenge. Andy is 66 years old. There is not a viable disability insurance policy that will pay in case he is unable to work due to a disability.

The business is currently a "C" corp, so all of Andy's income must either be compensation (an expense of the business) or dividends (earnings of the business). Restructuring the business to an "S" corp may allow Andy to receive income in spite of a disability that will not trigger the double taxation of dividend payments.

CONCLUSION

The values that you pass along, the wealth that goes to a new generation, and the principles you perpetuate as you leave your business to another, are of momentous significance to your family. You are stewards of a wide-ranging family fortune comprised of values, morals, principles, and money. Others will follow your commendable example, if all has been handled correctly. Though, on the surface, this decision appears to be purely about money and business management, it is more notably about people and the legacy you have chosen to entrust.

part 7
APPENDIX A: workbook

> ## What do I want to achieve during my lifetime?

<u>What would I like to do over the next three years?</u>

If I knew I had only six months to live, what would I make sure to accomplish before then?

LEGACY BY DESIGN

PLANNING TOOLS

Rank each in level of importance & priority...   (1-low, 5-high)
Business Goals:
1. To ensure that the farm/agribusiness remains in the family.

_____

2. To make the transition to new ownership/management transparent to our customers, clients, strategic alliances, and third
party vendors.   _____
3. To minimize the cost/associated expense of transition.   _____
4. Other: _____
    Notes:

Ownership Succession:
1. To transfer ownership within _____ years.   _____
2. To ensure that loyal employees are offered an opportunity for
continued employment and/or the opportunity of an ownership
interest.   _____
3. If a partnership, to acquire other interest if/when available.

4. To minimize income tax due to ownership transition.   _____

5. To receive fair market value for ownership interest if sold.   _____

6. To continue receiving an income following transition.   _____

7. To reduce exposure to business liabilities.   _____
8. Avoid gift tax, minimize estate tax and transfer obligations.

9. Other: _____
    Notes:

Management Succession:
1. To transition to new management in _____ years.   _____
2. To transition management control to _____

3. In case of premature death or disability _____ should   _____
continue to run the operation until _____ is ready to
assume the role.
4. Other: _____
Notes:

270

Wealth Accumulation:
1. To develop an investment program.   _____
2. To protect assets through contingency planning.   _____
3. To provide a college education for children/grandchildren.

4. Leave a meaningful legacy to _____ organization.   _____

5. Other: _____
   Notes:

Retirement or the next venture in your vocational life:
1. To accumulate an investment portfolio that I cannot outgrow.

                                                        _____
2. To retire by/on _____.   _____
3. To move on to the next venture in my vocational life by _____.

                                                        _____
4. To provide an income of $_____ adjusted for inflation.

                                                        _____
5. Other: _____
Notes:

Estate Planning:
1. To efficiently pass the assets of my estate.   _____
2. To minimize estate tax and transfer obligations.   _____
3. To contribute to _____ charitable bequest.   _____
4. To provide for the special needs of _____.   _____
5. Other: _____
   Notes:

BUSINESS PLANNING

Can you articulate a clear, concise, vision for your farm/ agribusiness? _____

Write a sentence that summarizes your vision _____
_____

Summarize Business:
<u>Strengths</u> to build on _____
_____

<u>Opportunities</u> for growth _____
_____

<u>Competition</u> to address _____
_____

<u>Weaknesses</u> that threaten success _____
_____

Write your top 3 business goals:
    1. :

    2. :

    3. :

What are the 3 most influential trends affecting your business, industry or customer?
    1. :

    2. :

    3. :

Estimated current business value $ _____

Projected value in 5 years $ _____

Projected value in 10 years $ _____

Explain positive/negative value trend _____
_____

Prioritize the following roles the business occupies in your family life (1 through 7):

___ Provide Income

___ Provide employment for family members

___ Provide family identity

___ Provide status in the community

___ Carry on family name/identity

___ Build multigenerational wealth

___ Provide a legacy for subsequent generations

A farm/agribusiness may represent significant family wealth. Prioritize the following roles wealth may occupy in your business/family life (1 through 7):

___ Provide funding for next venture in vocational life.

___ Provide adequate income for surviving spouse/ dependents.

___ Provide for the education of children/ grandchildren.

___ Provide financial support for children/ grandchildren.

___ Care for aging parents.

___ Support charitable organization(s).

___ Establish a charitable trust/foundation.

Name one factor, concern, goal, or consideration that is not up for compromise: _____
_____

SUCCESSION QUESTIONS TO CONSIDER

1. Is planning for succession important?
2. Is your business plan designed to facilitate a succession plan?
3. Is your family prepared, informed, and supportive?
4. Will you consider related as well as unrelated successors?
5. Is company ownership titled for succession?
6. Have you designed a plan for candidate development?
7. Have you considered a board of directors or a family council?
8. Have you arranged for equitable transfers to passive heirs?
9. Do you have a contingency plan for spousal support?
10. Have you thoroughly communicated your succession intentions, and developed a communication process for each phase of implementation?

LEADERSHIP SKILLS INVENTORY

Business Operations Skills	Level 1-5	Leadership Skills	Level 1-5
Recognizes potential problems and attempts to troubleshoot		Promotes a sense of team	
Develops and demonstrates good safety habits		Promotes a positive working	
Performs well at all duties and responsibilities		Recognizes potential areas of conflict and initiates mitigation	
Exhibits patience and clarity in training others		Understands and demonstrates a dedication to quality	
Completes outside training to improve job skills		Performs as an integral part of a team	
Demonstrates good use of computer/electronic tools and processes		Demonstrates good business etiquette with others (internal and external customers)	
Utilizes good business systems/processes		Utilizes good people development skills	
Understands business plan and can implement accordingly		Maintains confidentiality when appropriate	
Utilizes excellent financial management skills		Deals objectively with employee interaction	
Can plan and budget for business growth/ development		Delegates with clear responsibility and holds others accountable	
Innovates to improve business systems/processes		Mentors others in leadership development	

Understands particular industry		Works as if success depends on his/her actions	
Judiciously utilizes limited resources		Develops good relationships w/employees, customers, etc.	

FINANCIAL PLANNING

Are you satisfied with your current level of savings/ investment? _____

If no, explain _____

Are satisfied with the returns your investment portfolio generates? _____

If no, explain _____

Are you satisfied with the current asset allocation of your portfolio? _____

If no, explain _____

If your $250,000 mutual fund portfolio decreased in value by 12% or $30,000 in one year how would you react?
  1. Sell, cut my losses and reinvest the balance elsewhere.
  2. Shift the allocation to a more conservative mix.
  3. Do nothing as I invest for the long-term.
  4. Buy more... I have an opportunity to buy low!

Do you understand the devastating ramifications of inflation, and do you factor inflation into your investment return expectations? _____
If no, explain _____

What lifestyle stage are you in?
Accumulation ___, Consolidation ___, Spending ___ or Gifting ___ phase.

Do you understand the six critical investment concepts? (Check if comfortable)
    ___1) The Importance of Asset Allocation
    ___2) Understanding Diversification
    ___3) Combining Dissimilar Investments
    ___4) Adding Time to Your Investment Program
    ___5) The Magic of Compounding
    ___6) Understanding Asset Class Investing

Is the assistance/advice of a financial services professional important to the success of your investment plan? _____
_____

If no, explain _____

THE LIFEBOAT DRILL EXERCISE

Assume you have $200,000 invested in the stock market. On your next monthly statement, you see that your $200,000 has become $194,000. Are you still on board? The next month, you're down to $188,000. Then it drops to $184,000. How are you feeling now? Are you still okay with doing nothing or are you getting your lifeboat ready? The month after that, it drops to $180,000. Then it goes down further to $170,000, $154,000, $130,000, and eventually to $100,000. At what point do you jump ship?

Potential Quarterly Decline	Original Investment $200,000	Check the box where you would take action
(3%)	$194,000	☐
(6%)	$188,000	☐
(8%)	$184,000	☐
(10%)	$180,000	☐
(15%)	$170,000	☐
(23%)	$154,000	☐
(35%)	$130,000	☐
(50%)	$100,000	☐

SIMPLIFIED DATA SHEET
(MATERIALS TO HAVE ON HAND IN
PREPARATION FOR SUCCESSION PLANNING)

The initial data gathering system may include the following questions or areas of interest:

1. Family census: names, residential and farm addresses, contact data (phone, fax, e-mail), names of children, grandchildren, ages and dates of birth for all family members, Social Security numbers, health status, special needs.
2. Net Worth Statement: ownership of all assets, i.e. ownership by you, your spouse or partner; joint ownership (define such as JTWROS, TIC, Community property, etc.); trust (define); other (define, such as accounts held for minors). Request copies of all statements.
3. Checking, savings, money market, CDs (including maturity date).
4. Farm real estate, including residence, additional properties. Identify owner, purchase price, current value, mortgage terms and current balance, cash flow from farm properties.
5. Farm partnerships (obtain copy of recent quarterly or annual report). Determine cash flow, tax benefits, estimated values, liquidity, if any.
6. Other farm related business interests: name; type of business; form of ownership (C-corp., S-corp., sole proprietor, partnership, LLC); percentage of ownership; value of interest; buy/sell agreement or succession plan.
7. Farm equipment/assets, age, value, current depreciation schedule, outstanding loans.

8. Personal assets: description (trucks, car, aircraft); value; debt. List value of other assets such as jewelry, household furnishings.

9. Retirement plans: obtain statements for all pension/profit sharing plans; IRAs; 401(k); deferred compensation plans, etc. Specify primary and contingent beneficiaries.

10. Stocks, bonds, mutual funds, (list or provide brokerage or custodial statement). Include data on U.S. Savings Bonds. Obtain tax basis for all securities.

11. Annuities (fixed and variable). Obtain copy of policy and recent quarterly and annual reports. Determine owner; annuitant; primary and contingent beneficiaries; tax status.

12. Life insurance. Request copy of policy, original proposal, and last annual statement. Determine type of policy, face amount, the insured, owner, beneficiary (primary and contingent), premium payments, adequacy of payments (how long will the policy carry given current assumptions?), purpose of the coverage, cash values if applicable (current value, surrender value, loans outstanding). Include data on group insurance and any coverage tied to employer benefits (if applicable).

13. Buy/sell agreements or business arrangements detail of the agreements, gather copies if available, source of funding, method of valuation, partners involved and degree of ownership.

14. Education planning: Section 529 Plans, Education IRAs, other.

15. Tangibles: type of asset (precious metals, gems, coins); date of purchase; original investment; current value.
16. Other insurance: copies of homeowner, rental, auto, umbrella liability policies; personal and group disability policies; long term care.
17. Copies of legal documents and other key documents: will(s); trusts (including revocable or irrevocable living trusts, charitable trusts); durable powers of attorney for assets and health care; divorce decrees, alimony and child support agreements; prenuptial agreements; purchase agreements; farm buy/sell agreements; family farming partnerships; most recent tax return.
18. Other advisors personal/professional: name, address, and contact information for other key advisors such as a CPA or other tax adviser; attorney, banker, trustees, insurance agents, brokers, etc.
19. Anything else you think is important to your life and future.

ESTATE PLANNING

Do you have a will? _____ Date _____ A living trust? _____
Date _____

Spouse have a will? _____ Date _____ A living trust? _____
Date _____

Do you have any other type of trust? _____ If yes, explain_
_____

Do you have charitable intentions? _____

If yes, explain _____

Do you intend equitable distributions to all your children?
                                          _____

If no, explain _____

Do you plan to provide college educations for your
children/grandchildren?
Who _____ How much? _____
Who _____ How much? _____
Who _____ How much? _____
Who _____ How much? _____

Do you anticipate supporting your parents (either/
both spouses), a special needs child or other person continuously in the future? _____

If yes, explain _____

Have you named an executor for your estate settlement
needs?   _____
Name: _____

Have you/spouse executed a health care durable power of attorney? _____

If no, explain _____

Is gifting to reduce estate taxes of interest to you now?
_____

Explain _____

Have you adequately provided for the financial security of your spouse? _____

Explain _____

LIFE INSURANCE NEEDS ANALYSIS

Life insurance provides money at the very time when it is needed most for:

Final Expenses	$_____
Outstanding Debts	$_____
Specific Needs	$_____
Educational Funds	$_____
Income Replacement	$_____
Business Overhead Fund	$_____
Estate Tax and Transfer Obligations	$_____
Administrative Expenses/Probate Fees	$_____
Equitable Transfer Fund	$_____
Total Life Insurance Required	$_____
Less: Current Life Insurance	<$_____>
LIFE INSURANCE SHORTFALL	$_____

RETIREMENT PLANNING

Do you plan to retire? _____ If so, when, and under what conditions? _____

Have you considered alternative ventures in your vocational life?   _____

If yes, explain _____

How much income do you need in retirement? _____

Total Cash Receipts	$	
Total Expenditures	$	
Retirement Deficit	-$	
Retirement Excess		+$

Do you have a deficit or an excess? _____

Can you build an accumulation plan?
   How much can you contribute? _____

   What rate of return should you assume? _____%

   How much time will you allow to reach your goal?

                                                      _____

Do you need to adjust one or more of your assumptions in order to realize your goal? _____

Explain _____

Should you consider a retirement plan that includes:

_____ Simplified Employee Pension	_____ Keogh
	_____ 401(k)
_____ Simple Plan	_____ Roth IRA
_____ IRA	_____ Annuity, Fixed/
_____ Defined Benefit Plan	Variable

What one lifetime goal is not open to compromise? ____

_____

Do you understand the four absolutes, if all else fails?

_____ Be an owner, not a loaner
_____ Do not try to time the markets
_____ Diversify your investment portfolio
_____ Do not panic

CASH NEEDS AT RETIREMENT:

		Current Expenses	Retirement Expenses
Housing	Mortgage payment		
	Utilities		
	Housing maintenance		
	Property insurance		
	Property taxes		
	Home furnishings		
Food and household expenses	Groceries		
	Household supplies		
Clothing	Clothing purchases		
	Cleaning		
Transportation	Automobile payments		
	Automobile insurance		
	Fuel, repairs, and parking		
Insurance (not property)	Health insurance		
	Life insurance		
	Liability insurance		
	Long-term care insurance		
Entertainment and recreation	Vacation and travel		

	Meals and other entertainment		
	Clubs and recreation		
Charitable contributions			
Debt repayment (not housing and automobile)	Credit card debt and outstanding bills		
	Installment notes		
	Rental or investment property		
	Other debt		
Miscellaneous expenses	Education		
	Gifts		
	Domestic help or landscaping		
	Alimony or child support		
	Professional expenses		
	Other		
Total Expenditures			

		Current Income	Retirement Income
Earned income	Husband		
	Wife		
Retirement plant/IRA distributions	Husband		
	Wife		
Social Security benefits	Husband		
	Wife		
Interest income			
Dividend income			
Royalty income	Husband		
	Wife		
Consultation income	Husband		
	Wife		
Other distributions			
Cash receipts	Sale of assets		
	Alimony or child support		
	Trust distributions		
	Other		
Total cash receipts			

INCOME AT RETIREMENT

SELECTING A PLANNER

1. Do you have experience providing advice on business succession planning and the following supporting areas?
    o   Business Planning
    o   Retirement Planning
    o   Estate Planning
    o   Investment Planning
    o   Insurance Planning
Notes: _____

_____

2. What qualifies you to act as a specialist in the field of business succession planning?
Notes: _____

_____

3. How long have you been offering business succession planning advice?
    o   Less than one year
    o   One to four years
    o   Five to ten years
    o   More than 10 years
Notes: _____

_____

4. For how many families do you currently provide business succession planning?
    o   Fewer than 10
    o   10 to 39
    o   40 to 79
    o   80 +
Notes: _____

5. Give me a brief overview of your career in financial services.
Notes: _____

_____

6. What are your educational qualifications? Briefly describe areas of study/specialization.
Notes: _____

_____

7. What financial planning designation(s) or certificate(s) do you hold?
   o Certified Financial Planner® (CFP®)
   o Certified Public Accountant-Personal Financial Specialist (CPA-PFS)
   o Chartered Financial Consultant (ChFC)
   o Other_____
Notes: _____

_____

8. Other than required continuing education hours, how many hours do you study regularly in your field of professional expertise?
Notes: _____

_____

9. What licenses do you hold?
   o Insurance
   o Securities
   o CPA
   o J.D. (Juris Doctorate: Attorney)
   o Other_____
Notes: _____

10. What services do you offer?
Notes: _____

_____

11. Briefly describe your approach to business
    succession planning.

Notes: _____

_____

12. Who will work directly with me?
    o   Planner
    o   Associate
Notes: _____

_____

13. Who will review my financial situation?
    o   Planner
    o   Associate
    o   Planning Dept. Personnel
    o   In-house Accountant(s)
    o   In-house Attorney(s)
Notes: _____

_____

14. How do you get paid for services? Do you fully
    disclose your compensation schedule?
    o   Fee
    o   Commission
    o   Salary
    o   Other

Notes: _____

15. Do you have strategic alliances with other complementary professionals to whom you may refer me, and do you receive a bonus or fee for the referral?
    o   Yes
    o   No
If yes, do you fully disclose this relationship and the bonus or fee?
    o   Yes
    o   No
Notes: _____

_____

16. Do you provide a written client engagement agreement?
    o   Yes
    o   No
Notes: _____

_____

GLOSSARY

The beginning of wisdom is to call things by their right names.

Advisor: A person who gives investment advice in return for compensation.

Analysis: Process of evaluating individual financial instruments to determine whether they are appropriate purchases.

Asset allocation: A mixture of investments distributed among various classes of financial instruments. The goal is to create a portfolio that provides the highest return for a given amount of risk. It can also reduce risk by placing portions of the portfolio in asset classes that move up or down in value in an inverse relationship one to another.

Asset class: Assets composed of financial instruments with similar characteristics.

Average return: The arithmetic mean is the simple average of the returns in a series.

Basis point: One basis point is 1/100th of a percentage point, or 0.01%. Basis points are often used to express changes or differences in yields, returns, or interest rates. Thus, if a portfolio has a total return of 10% versus 7% for the Standard & Poor's 500 (S&P 500) Index, the portfolio is said to have outperformed the S&P 500 Index by 300 basis points.

Bear market: A prolonged period of declining stock values. Wall Street defines a bear market as a drop of at least 20% over two back-to-back quarters.

Bequest: Leaving property to another person through a last will and testament.

Book-to-market ratio: Size of company's book (net) value relative to the market price of the company stocks.

Book value: The current value of an asset on a company's balance sheet according to its accounting conventions. The shareholders' equity on a company's balance sheet is the book value for that entire company.

Broker-dealer: A firm (intermediary) transacting buying and selling activities in investment markets through appointed brokers (financial professionals).

Bull market: A prolonged period of increasing stock values. Wall Street defines a bull market as a rise of at least 15% over two back-to-back quarters.

Cap (small cap, large cap): A term of reference used to categorize the capitalization of individual businesses.

Capital appreciation or depreciation: An increase or decrease in the value of a mutual fund or stock due to a change in the market price of the fund. If you bought a stock at $50 and it has risen to $55, you have a 10% return from the appreciation of the original capital you invested. If the price of the stock fell to $45, it would have a depreciation of 10%. Dividend yield is the other component of total return but not included in appreciation.

Capital preservation: Conservatively investing in an effort to minimize risk, thereby preserving capital.

Cash: An investment in any instrument that is easily liquidated.

Commodity: Basic items or staple products with little or no discernible difference between one producer/manufacturer and another.

Commoditization: The act or process of becoming a commodity. The danger of commoditization from an individual business perspective is a complete loss of differentiation and the opportunity to charge and, therefore, profit from your difference.

Compound interest: Interest paid on both the principal and the undistributed (accumulated) interest. The magic of compounding interest has a multiplying effect on investment returns.

Compounding: Reinvesting dividends, interest, and capital gains for an exponential return on investments. The formula for compound interest is: compound sum = principal (1+ interest rate) number of periods.

Conservative: There is no precise financial definition of the term. Generally, the term is used when the mutual fund manager's, or an investor's, emphasis is on the low-risk investments.

Corpus: The principal, not the income, interest, or dividend, of an investment, trust, or property of an estate.

Correlation: A statistical measure of the degree to which the movement of two variables is related.

Decedent: One who has passed away. Used in settling the estate, as in: "The decedent left all of his possessions to his son."

Diversification (the concept of): A simplified concept of diversification is "Don't put all your eggs in one basket." However, no matter how sophisticated we try to be, it is easy to favor one particular "basket." Many investors have a disproportionate percentage of their investment portfolio in one asset class. The true measure of diversification is not how many different investments you have, rather the degree of negative correlation of the investments in your portfolio.

Investments that move in the same direction tend to increase portfolio risk and reduce predictability. When investments are combined that move differently in time, in proportion, or in direction (dissimilar price movement), you have the basis for effective diversification.

Dow Jones Industrial Average (DJIA): A price-weighted average of 30 leading blue-chip industrial stocks, calculated by adding the prices of the 30 stocks and adjusting by a divisor, which reflects any stock dividends or splits. The Dow Jones Industrial Average is the most widely quoted index of the stock market, but it is not widely used as a benchmark for evaluating performance. The S&P 500 Index, which is more representative of the market, is the benchmark most widely used by performance measurement services.

Dividend: The payment from a company's earnings normally paid on common shares declared by a company's board of directors to be distributed pro rata among the shares outstanding.

Equities (stocks): A certificate of partial ownership in a corporation. The shorthand name for stocks and stock mutual funds is equities.

Fiduciary: A person who holds something in trust or acts in the best interest of another.

Fund shares: Shares in a mutual fund.

Index fund: A passively managed portfolio designed to replicate the performance of a certain index, such as the S&P 500 Index. In general, such mutual funds have performance results within a few basis points of the target index. The most popular index mutual funds are those that track the S&P 500, but special index funds, such as those based on the Russell 1000 or the Wilshire 5000, are also available.

Inflation: A monetary phenomenon generated by an over-expansion of credit which drives up prices of assets while diminishing the worth of paper currency.

Interest: The rate a borrower pays a lender.

Inter vivos: Usually associated with a living trust, as from one living person to another.

Intestate: Not disposed of by will, such as settling an estate without a will.

Invest: Disciplined process of placing money in financial instruments so as to gain a return. Given the emergence of valid academic research regarding asset-class investment methods, an individual who depends mostly on active management and stock-picking may be come to be considered a speculator rather than an investor.

Investment objective: The financial goals one wishes to reach.

Investment policy: An investment policy statement forces the investor to confront risk tolerance, return objectives, timeline, liquidity needs, the amount of funds available for investment, and the investment methodology to be followed.

Irrevocable: Something that cannot be revoked, recalled, or undone. It is unalterable.

Liquidity: Ability to generate cash on demand when necessary.

Maturities: Applies to bonds, the date at which a borrower must redeem the capital portion of his loan.

Market: In investing terms: a place where securities are traded. Formerly meant a physical location but now may refer to an electronic one as well.

Model portfolio: A theoretical construct of an investment or series of investments.

Modern Portfolio Theory: Professor Harry Markowitz built an investment strategy that took more than 30 years to develop; it is recognized as Modern Portfolio Theory. He won the Nobel Prize for his work in 1990.

Mutual fund: Investment companies that continually offer new shares and redeem (buy back) existing shares at the request of shareholder's. It uses its capital to invest in diversified securities of other companies, according to the investment objectives stated in the prospectus.

Management fee: Charge against investor assets for managing the portfolio of an open- or closed-end mutual fund. The fee, as disclosed in the prospectus, is a fixed percentage of the fund's asset value, typically 1% or less a year.

Market value: Is the market or liquidation value of a given security or of an entire pool of assets.

Mutual fund families: A mutual fund sponsor or company usually offers a number of funds with different investment objectives within its family of funds. For example, a mutual fund family may include a money market fund, a government bond fund, a corporate bond fund, a blue chip stock fund, and a more speculative stock fund. If an investor buys a fund in the family, he or she is allowed to exchange that fund for another in the same family.

Net asset value (NAV): This is defined as the market value of each share of a mutual fund. This figure is derived by taking a fund's total assets (securities, cash and receivables), deducting liabilities, and then dividing that total by the number of shares outstanding.

Nominal return: The actual current dollar growth in an asset's value over a given period.

Portfolio: A collection of investments held by an investor, investment company, or financial institution.

Probate: Settling a will. Probate is subject to public scrutiny.

Principal: The original dollar amount invested.

Prospectus: The document required by the Securities and Exchange Commission that accompanies the sale of a mutual fund or annuity outlining risks associated with certain types of funds or securities, fees, and management. At the core of the prospectus is a description of the fund's investment objectives and the portfolio manager's philosophy.

Rate of return: The profits earned by a security as measured as a percentage of earned interest (dividends) or appreciation.

Rebalancing: Is a process whereby funds are shifted within asset classes and between asset classes to insure the maintenance of the efficient frontier.

Real return: This is the inflation-adjusted return on an asset. Inflation-adjusted returns are calculated by subtracting the rate of inflation from an asset's apparent, or nominal, return. For example, if common stocks earn a total return of 10.3% over a period of time, but inflation during that period is 3.1 percent, the real return is the difference: 7.2%.

Revocable: Something that can be revoked, recalled or undone. It is alterable.

Reinvested dividends: It refers to dividends paid by a particular mutual fund that are reinvested in that same mutual fund. Some mutual funds offer automatic dividend reinvestment programs.

Risk: Risk is nothing more than the uncertainty of future rates of return, which includes the possibility of loss.

Risk tolerance: Investors' innate ability to deal with the potential of losing money without abandoning their investment plan.

ROI: Return on investment, the amount of money generated over time by placement of funds in specific financial instruments.

S&P 500 Index: The performance benchmark most widely used by sponsors, managers, and performance measurement services. This index includes 400 industrial stocks, 20 transportation stocks, 40 financial stocks, and 40 public utilities.

Securities and Exchange Commission (SEC): The keystone law in the regulation of securities markets. It governs exchanges, over-the-counter markets, broker-dealers, the conduct of secondary markets, extension of credit in securities transactions, the conduct of corporate insiders, and principally the prohibition of fraud and manipulation in securities transactions. It also outlines the powers of the Securities and Exchange Commission to interpret, supervise, and enforce the securities laws of the United States.

Securities: A tradable financial instrument.

Shares: Specific portions of tradable equity.

Standard deviation: Standard deviation describes how far from the mean historic performance has been, either higher or lower. Mean is simply the middle point between the two historic extremes of the performance of the investment you are examining. The standard deviation measurement helps explain what the distribution of returns likely will be. The greater the range of returns, the greater the risk; the lower the risk, the lower the return expected.

Stock: A contract signifying ownership or a portion of a public or private company.

Succession: The process by which a business owner transitions the business to the next owner (generation).

Testamentary: As in a trust formed after death through a will.

Timeline: The amount of time someone can wait to generate income or take profits from an investment.

Total return: A standard measure of performance or return including both capital appreciation (depreciation) and dividends or other income received.

Volatility: The extent to which market values and investment returns are uncertain or fluctuate.

BIBLIOGRAPHY

Agricultural Statistics Board. *Farms and Land in Farms.* Washington, DC: National Agricultural Statistics Service, United States Department of Agriculture, February 2004.

Allen M. *Visionary Business.* Novato, CA: New World Library, 1997.

Anders G. Farmers and sons, at potato empire: an heir peels away years of tradition. *The Wall Street Journal.* October 7, 2004.

Associated Press. Ag women breaking through 'glass ceiling.' *Capital Press.* April 30, 2004.

Arzt RA, Stork DG. *Retirement Planning.* Bethesda, MD: The Life Underwriter Training Council, 1998.

Astrachan JH, Shanker MC. Myths and realities: family businesses' contribution to the U. S. economy. *Family Business Review.* Summer 1996.

Astrachan JH, Shanker MC. Family businesses' contribution to the U. S. economy: a closer look. *Family Business Review.* September 2003.

Avila SM, Avila RA, Naffziger DW. A comparison of family-owned businesses: succession planners and nonplanners. *Journal of Financial Services Professionals.* April 2003.

Ayers GR. Budgeting for continuity. *Family Business Magazine.* Spring 1998.

Bay A. Farming for the love of it. *Capital Press*. September 3, 2000.

Bergman VR, Lovelace TW, McMurrian SS, Smith BT. *Business Ownership and Management Succession*. Vols. I and II. Fort Worth, TX: Thomson Practitioners Publishing Company, 2004.

Black P. Planning your estate, don't let your wealth blow away. *Smart Money*. November 2003.

Boehje MD, Hofing SL, Schroeder RC. Farming in the 21st century. Department of Agricultural Economics, Purdue University, West Lafayette, Indiana; Agricultural Education and Consulting, August 31, 1999.

Bowie M. Workers promised their own company. *St. Petersburg Times*. March 26, 2004.

Bradley Dalton JF, Dalton MA. Dalton Review for the CFP Certification Examination, 6th ed. St. Rose, LA: Dalton Publications, 2002.

Brawer R. Running away from succession. *Family Business Magazine*. Spring 1999.

Brown JH, Durnford JM. The role of the financial advisor in helping owners leave their businesses in style. *Journal of Financial Services Professionals*. December 1998.

Buford B. *Half Time: Changing Your Game Plan from Success to Significance*. Grand Rapids, MI: Zondervan Publishing, 1994.

Certified Financial Planning Board of Standards. Financial planning process. Denver, Colorado: Certified Financial Planning Board of Standards, 2003.

Certified Financial Planning Board of Standards. Checklist for interviewing a financial planner. Denver, Colorado: Certified Financial Planning Board of Standards, 2003.

Chambers L, Rogers D. *The First Time Investor,* 3rd ed. New York, NY: McGraw-Hill, 2004.

Cherney E, Frank R. A brewing family feud poses risks for Molson Beer empire. *The Wall Street Journal.* June 29, 2004.

Cohn M, Rottenberg D. Openers, case study: the impatient daughter-in-law. *Family Business Magazine.* Winter 2001.

Cohn M Doud E. The top ten excuses for not letting go. *Family Business Magazine.* Summer 1994.

Cohn M. Are you planning to pass the torch? *Family Business Magazine.* Summer 1995.

Danco L, Nager RW. The 10 deadly sins in estate planning. *Family Business Magazine.* Spring 1993.

Danco L. Widows who become pilots without ever flying. *Family Business Magazine.* Spring 1993.

Editorial Staff. Family business in the U. S. *Family Business Review*, 2000.

Editors of Family Business Magazine. *The Family Business Succession Handbook.* Philadelphia, PA: Family Business Publishing, 2001.

Esperti RA, Peterson RL. *Protect Your Estate*, 2nd ed. New York, NY: McGraw-Hill, 2000.

Field A. After the windfall. *Worth*. September 2004.

Fishkind RJ, Kautz RC. *Estate and Business Succession Planning*, 2nd ed. New York, NY: John Wiley, 2002.

Flynn J. Inside a Napa Valley empire, a family struggles with itself. *The Wall Street Journal*. June 3, 2004.

Frankenberg E. What family businesses are not. *Family Business Magazine*. Spring 2003.

Garry R, Garry S. Family business background. *Journal of Financial Services Professionals*. May 1998.

Geller DL, Krinkle TD, White WS. Family business succession planning: devising an overall strategy. *Journal of Financial Services Professionals*. May 2004.

Heimer M. The new retirement. *Smart Money*. April 2004.

Hillyer G. Smooth transition. *Progressive Farmer*. August 2003.

Horan PJ. Establishing an advisory board for the family business. *Journal of Financial Services Professionals*. November 2003.

Howe RF. The fall of the house of Mondavi. *Business 2.0*. April 2005.

Hulme FS, Loeb,ME, Potts TL, Schoen JE. Effective retirement for family business owner-managers, Parts I and 2. *Journal of Financial Planning.* July 2001.

Jaffe DT. Strategic planning for the family in business. *Journal of Financial Planning.* March 2005.

Jonovic D, Messick W. *Passing Down the Farm.* Cleveland, OH: Jamieson Press, 1996.

Jurinski JJ. Family limited partnerships: a primer on the risks and rewards. *Journal of Financial Services Professionals.* May 2004.

Kilman S. Moving on up. *The Wall Street Journal.* November 8, 2004.

Koiranen M. Understanding the contesting ideologies of family business. *Family Business Review.* December 2003.

Kramer M. *Three Farms Making Milk, Meat, and Money from the American Soil.* New York, NY: Bantam Books, 1981.

Lakein A. *How to Get Control of Your Time and Your Life.* New York, NY: Signet-NAL Publishing, 1973.

Lane SH, Jaffe DT. Sustaining a family dynasty: key issues facing complex multigenerational business. *Family Business Review.* March 2004.

Looker D. Estate tax planning gets more complicated. *Successful Farming.* February 2005.

Malkiel BG. *A Random Walk Down Wall Street.* New York, NY: Norton & Company, 1973.

Mass Mutual Financial Group/Raymond Institute. American family business survey. Mass Mutual Life Insurance Company, January 22, 2003.

Mowitz D. Amazing future. *Successful Farming*. February 2005.

Murray N. *Simple Wealth, Inevitable Wealth*. Mattituck, NY: Nick Murray Company, 1999.

Opdyke JD. *Struggling to retire on $1 Million*. The Wall Street Journal. September 17, 2004.

Power C. Premiums challenge organic growers. *Capital Press*. April 23, 2004.

Rawls L. Pushing parents into succession. *Family Business Magazine*. Summer 2000.

Renkert-Thomas A. Fifth-generation family secrets. *Family Business Magazine*. Spring 2004.

Rogers MF. Buy-sell planning for second and subsequent generation owners. *Journal of Financial Services Professionals*. March 2004.

Rottenberg D. Contrarian's notebook, estate tax: a blessing in disguise. *Family Business Magazine*. Autumn 2000.

Rukeyser MS. *The Common Sense of Money and Investments*. New York, NY: John Wiley & Sons, 1999.

Saccacio J. Moving out. *Investment Advisor Magazine*. July 2003.

Schueller MP, Tolan DJ. The interpersonal dynamics of business succession planning. *Journal of Financial Services Professionals.* July 1994.

Siegel J. *Stocks for the Long Run.* 3rd ed. New York, NY: McGraw-Hill, 2002.

Smith RA. Making family limited partnerships IRS friendly. *The Wall Street Journal.* January 7, 2004.

Sobol MR, Solum RS, Wall B. *The Visionary Leader.* Rocklin, CA: Prima Publishing, 1992.

Stevick GE Jr. *Essentials of Business Insurance.* Bryn Mawr, PA: American College, 2003.

Steward P. Caring for cattle and the land. *Capital Press.* April 23, 2004.

Stone D. Succession journeys. *Family Business Magazine.* Autumn 1999.

Taylor C. Permanent vacation. *Smart Money.* July 2004.

Tevis C. Heart attack is estate planning wake-up call. *Successful Farming.* February 2005.

Tevis C. How this farm family plans for long-term success. *Successful Farming.* February 2005.

Tevis C. Farm transfer linked to policy, succession is challenged by economic trends and government policies. *Successful Farming.* December 2003.

Updegrave W. Retirement storm clouds. *Money*. November 2003.

Weikart RJ, Williams RC. *Foundations of Estate Planning.* Bryn Mawr, PA: American College, 2002.

Widhalm EL. Effects of succession planning on stress, life satisfaction, and self-esteem in two-generation farm families. A Thesis for Master of Science in Home Economics. Bozeman, MT: Montana State University, August 1990.

RESOURCE GUIDE
Recommended Reading

The Life Insurance Handbook
By Louis S. Shuntich

Term Life insurance, Whole Life insurance, Variable and Universal Life insurance – the list of choices for insurance products continues to grow, along with the different uses and tax implications associated with each. Despite the dizzying pace of change in the industry, every financial professional must understand the different types of insurance available – and the considerations for purchasing them.

$19.95   Item# BC105x1611783

LIFE INSURANCE IN ACTION SET WITH 25Q
By Dearborn Financial Publishing

This text provides an understanding of the ways life insurance offers financial stability and protection against the financial constraints of death. It explains the many applications of life insurance products and how their flexibility allows them to cover a wide range of clients' needs.

$29.00   Item# BC105x1834687

LIFE AND HEALTH INSURANCE, 13TH EDITION
By Kenneth Black and Harold D. Skipper

In this newly revised thirteenth edition, the authors continue their emphasis on combining current information about life and health insurance products and their uses with careful consideration of the environment. They also carry on approaching their presentation of life and health insurance simultaneously from the viewpoints of the buyer, the advisor, and the insurer. This outstanding book is an informative guide to all the ins and outs of life and health insurance.

$133.00   Item# BC105x12530

NEW LIFE INSURANCE INVESTMENT ADVISOR: ACHIEVING FINANCIAL SECURITY FOR YOU AND YOUR FAMILY THROUGH TODAY'S INSURANCE PRODUCTS, 2ND EDITION
By Ben G. Baldwin

This book is one of the most authoritative resources on today's highly dynamic, versatile, and adaptable investment vehicle. It covers Term Life, Whole Life, Universal Life, Variable Life insurance – and more. Discover the benefits of each for various client scenarios and life goals – and learn how to apply them when building stable portfolios. From finding optimal insurance products for different life stages to innovative techniques for using the capital hidden in each policy – this is the definitive book on the topic.

$29.95   Item# BC105x41593

INVESTMENT GUARANTEES: MODELING AND RISK MANAGEMENT FOR EQUITY-LINKED LIFE INSURANCE
By Mary Hardy

Whether you are involved with product design, marketing, pricing and valuation, or risk management of equity-linked insurance, this book has something for you. It combines the econometric analysis of these investment models with their applications in pricing and risk management. Filled with professional insights and proven techniques, this comprehensive guide is a valuable one-stop reference that will allow you to better understand the theory and practice behind modeling and risk management for equity-linked life insurance

$95.00   Item# BC105x956602

THE COMPLETE GUIDE TO COMPENSATION PLANNING WITH LIFE INSURANCE
By Louis S. Shuntich

Help your clients attract and retain high caliber employees with this new and compact reference guide. An ideal educational tool for today's information-hungry and time-strapped professional, this book includes an overview of the various compensation plans available, the many features each plan offers, and a summary of how they compare and can be applied to different scenarios.

$29.95   Item# BC105x1611782

PASSTRAK LIFE INSURANCE: LICENSE EXAM MANUAL
By Dearborn Financial Publishing

This course surveys life insurance principles and concepts common to all state producer licensing exams. It is intended as a comprehensive introduction to life insurance. Topics include contract law, life insurance policies, premiums and proceeds, underwriting and policy issue, group life insurance, annuities, retirement plans, and more. The book further contains lesson objectives and special notes. It is clear, complete, up-to-date, and consists of revised forms and the NAIFA Code of Ethics. An index is included to make this text more useful as a study and reference tool.

$26.00   Item# BC105x758345

Free 2 Week Trial Offer for U.S. Residents From Investor's Business Daily:

INVESTOR'S BUSINESS DAILY will provide you with the facts, figures, and objective news analysis you need to succeed.

Investor's Business Daily is formatted for a quick and concise read to help you make informed and profitable decisions.

This book, along with other books, is available at discounts that make it realistic to provide it as a gift to your customers, clients, and staff. For more information on these long lasting, cost effective premiums, please call us at (800) 272-2855 or you may email us at sales@fpbooks.com.